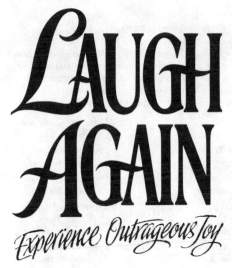

# LAUGH AGAIN

*Experience Outrageous Joy*

A STUDY OF PHILIPPIANS

## BIBLE STUDY GUIDE

From the Bible-teaching ministry of

*Charles R. Swindoll*

INSIGHT FOR LIVING

Charles R. Swindoll is a graduate of Dallas Theological Seminary and has served as senior pastor of the First Evangelical Free Church of Fullerton, California, since 1971. Chuck's radio program, "Insight for Living," began in 1979. In addition to his church and radio ministries, Chuck enjoys writing. He has authored numerous books and booklets on a variety of subjects.

Based on the outlines and transcripts of Chuck's sermons, the study guide text is co-authored by Lee Hough, a graduate of the University of Texas at Arlington and Dallas Theological Seminary. He also wrote the Living Insights sections.

| | |
|---|---|
| **Editor in Chief:**<br>Cynthia Swindoll | **Director, Communications Division:**<br>Deedee Snyder |
| **Coauthor of Text:**<br>Lee Hough | **Project Manager:**<br>Alene Cooper |
| **Assistant Editor:**<br>Wendy Peterson | **Project Supervisor:**<br>Susan Nelson |
| **Copy Editors:**<br>Deborah Gibbs,<br>Glenda Schlahta | **Project Assistants:**<br>Ellen Galey,<br>Cheryl Gilmore |
| **Production Artist:**<br>Alex Pasieka | **Print Production Manager:**<br>John Norton |
| **Typographer:**<br>Bob Haskins | **Printer:**<br>Sinclair Printing Company |

Unless otherwise identified, all Scripture references are from the New American Standard Bible, © The Lockman Foundation 1960, 1962, 1963, 1968, 1971, 1972, 1973, 1975, 1977. Used by permission. Other translations cited are the Good News Bible [GNB], The Living Bible [LB], and J.B. Phillips: The New Testament in Modern English [PHILLIPS].

An effort has been made to locate sources and obtain permission where necessary for the quotations used in this book. In the event of any unintentional omission, a modification will gladly be incorporated in future printings.

ISBN 0-8499-8434-3
Printed in the United States of America.

# CONTENTS

# INTRODUCTION

I am not the first to point out that the letter Paul wrote to the Philippians is a letter of joy, and there isn't a more important character trait needed today. Joy is the Christian's most obvious advertisement that he or she has something that can make a difference in life. Joy is the flag flown over the castle of our heart announcing the King is in residence.

When the angels appeared to the shepherds near Bethlehem shortly after Jesus' birth, they called their message "good news of great joy." *And so it is!* But somehow we have forgotten the value of a joyful countenance. For some strange reason we have lost the fun in this life of faith . . . the contagious magnet of inner happiness has grown weak. As a close friend of mine often says to his congregation, "Many of you are happy down deep . . . but your face hasn't found it out yet!"

My hope is that this delightful little four-chapter book will help bring back your joy and remind you of the importance of letting it flow. It shouldn't be long before your face will show it!

Chuck Swindoll

# PUTTING TRUTH
# INTO ACTION

Knowledge apart from application falls short of God's desire for His children. He wants us to apply what we learn so that we will change and grow. This study guide was prepared with these goals in mind. As you go through the following pages, we hope your desire to discover biblical truth will grow as your understanding of God's Word increases, and that you will be encouraged to apply what you've learned.

To assist you in your study, we've included a section called **Living Insights** at the end of each lesson. These exercises will challenge you to study further and to think of specific ways to put your discoveries into action.

There are many ways to use this guide—in personal devotions, group studies, discussions with friends and family, and Sunday school classes. And, of course, it's an ideal study aid when you're listening to its corresponding "Insight for Living" radio series.

To benefit most from this study guide, we would encourage you to consider it a spiritual journal. That's why we've included space in the **Living Insights** for recording your thoughts and discoveries. We hope you'll return to those sections often for review and encouragement as you continue to grow in your walk with Christ.

Lee Hough
Coauthor of Text
Author of Living Insights

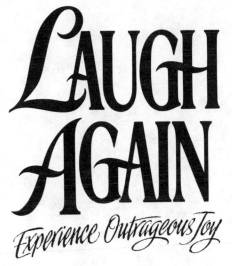

# LAUGH AGAIN

*Experience Outrageous Joy*

## A STUDY OF PHILIPPIANS

# YOUR SMILE INCREASES YOUR FACE VALUE

### A Survey of Philippians

Otters know about joy. They know how to take life by the throat, how to live every dip, swirl, slide down a mud bank to the fullest. There is no tomorrow or last week, only a joyous, playful present. Those lithe, brown bolts of energy took Thoreau seriously and sucked all the marrow out of life, leaving the business of leading lives of quiet desperation to the rest of us.[1] They have even figured a way to make us pay just to watch them play. This is highway robbery!

But what can we do? Arrest them? Probably wouldn't do any good. They'd just bring their joy with them—like the apostle Paul. He was arrested once in Philippi, then beaten with rods, and then thrown into prison with his feet locked in stocks. Come midnight, however, that battered Apostle had every tormented prisoner within earshot listening intently as he prayed and sang praises to God (Acts 16:22–25).

That's joy. Pure, unalloyed, magnetic. The kind you don't see very often nowadays—except in otters. It's certainly not in the newspapers or nightly news. It's not even in many churches. Have you noticed the looks on the average Sunday morning crowd? One word comes to mind—grim. There they are: rows of overcast faces whose forecast is for dreary to mildly depressing days, with little or no chance of any laughter.

But let's be fair—it's not just churchgoers. Ours is a world of long faces and aching hearts crying for a morsel of joy, a crumb of

---

1. Henry David Thoreau, *Walden*, as quoted by Sculley Bradley, Richmond Croom Beatty, and E. Hudson Long, eds., in *The American Tradition in Literature*, 4th ed. (New York, N.Y.: Putnam Publishing Group, Grosset and Dunlap, 1974), vol. 1, pp. 1224, 1280.

encouragement. It's just that you would expect believers, of all people, to exhibit a contagious and enthusiastic joy. One that even an otter might pay to come see. The kind that has little difficulty convincing nonbelievers that Christ *can* make a difference in life.

How can we tap into that kind of joy—the kind that makes our Christianity contagious even during times of crisis? Is it possible? Well, as you might expect, the otters aren't telling. But Paul does, in a simple yet profound letter of joy written to the Christians in Philippi, the same Roman colony where he had been arrested and beaten once before.

From start to finish, the enthusiastic joy and encouragement Paul poured out to those Philippian believers surely made them smile. And, by God's grace, this letter still has the power to teach us how to smile, how to take life by the throat, how to live every dip, swirl, slide down a mud bank to the fullest!

## Read a Letter with a Surprising Theme

Of all the New Testament letters, Philippians is one of the simplest. It measures only 104 verses long, and the theology is easy to grasp. Still, it is quite a catch—if we don't make the mistake of attempting to dissect each verb, noun, and adjective. This is a letter, remember, not an academic treatise. And Paul's joy is an emotion to be expressed, not an equation to be analyzed. Perhaps the profound truth of it all will be best caught if we enjoy Philippians for what it is, a letter from one friend to another.

### In a Single Word

Sometimes it's difficult to capture the essence of a letter in one word, but as you've probably already guessed, the heart of Philippians is *joy*. Paul didn't write to answer any profound questions or to solve knotty problems or even to deal with a particular sin. Instead, he wrote to express joy and encourage joy in dear friends— like Lydia, his first convert in Philippi, and the Roman jailer, who washed Paul's wounds and gave him food to eat (see Acts 16).

### Woven through Each Chapter

Let's take a brief tour of Philippians, where you'll see for yourself how Paul's buoyant joy keeps rising to the surface in each chapter.

Chapter 1 opens with Paul's cheerful admission that his prayers for the Philippians always kindle a joy in his heart.

I thank my God in all my remembrance of you, always offering prayer with joy in my every prayer for you all. (vv. 3–4)

Later in this same chapter, Paul reveals the conflicting desires in his heart that have led him to stir up the Philippians' joy in the faith.

But I am hard-pressed from both directions, having the desire to depart and be with Christ, for that is very much better; yet to remain on in the flesh is more necessary for your sake. And convinced of this, I know that I shall remain and continue with you all for your progress and joy in the faith. (vv. 23–25)

Crossing over into chapter 2, the Apostle encourages the Philippians to work together in harmony and, by doing so, enrich his own joy.

If therefore there is any encouragement in Christ, if there is any consolation of love, if there is any fellowship of the Spirit, if any affection and compassion, make my joy complete by being of the same mind, maintaining the same love, united in spirit, intent on one purpose. (vv. 1–2)

Joy resurfaces again a few verses later as Paul exhorts the church at Philippi to welcome back the faithful friend they had sent to him.

But I thought it necessary to send to you Epaphroditus, my brother and fellow worker and fellow soldier, who is also your messenger and minister to my need; because he was longing for you all and was distressed because you had heard that he was sick. For indeed he was sick to the point of death, but God had mercy on him, and not on him only but also on me, lest I should have sorrow upon sorrow. Therefore I have sent him all the more eagerly in order that when you see him again you may rejoice and I may be less concerned about you. Therefore receive him in the Lord with all joy, and hold men like him in high regard. (vv. 25–29)

Now let's move on to chapter 3, where Paul reminds the Philippians to find their joy in the Lord.

Finally, my brethren, rejoice in the Lord. (v. 1a)

Next, in chapter 4, Paul repeats this command:

> Rejoice in the Lord always; again I will say, rejoice! (v. 4)

And last, Paul mentions the great joy he feels because of the Philippians' care and concern.

> But I rejoiced in the Lord greatly, that now at last you have revived your concern for me; indeed, you were concerned before, but you lacked opportunity. (v. 10)

Altogether, the word *joy* and its derivative *rejoice* are mentioned sixteen times throughout this contagiously upbeat letter. A letter that becomes even more intriguing as you discover who wrote it, what sort of people received it, and why it was written in the first place.

## Understanding Some Background Information

For a letter to express such joy, you would be tempted to think that the author wrote it while sunning himself on the polished deck of a Mediterranean luxury liner. But nothing could be further from the truth.

### Who Wrote the Letter?

We know from Philippians 1:1 that Paul authored this epistle with the assistance of his close companion Timothy.[2] And we're also told in chapter 1 that Paul wrote it while imprisoned.

> Now I want you to know, brethren, that my circumstances have turned out for the greater progress of the gospel, so that my imprisonment in the cause of Christ has become well known throughout the whole praetorian guard and to everyone else, and that most of the brethren, trusting in the Lord because of my imprisonment, have far more courage to speak the word of God without fear. (vv. 12–14)

Paul was under house arrest in Rome, which meant he was constantly chained at the wrist to a Roman guard (see also Acts 28:16). Still, nothing could bind the joy Christ had given him for the church at Philippi.

2. Timothy was with Paul when he established the church at Philippi on his second missionary journey (see Acts 16).

### What Kind of People Received It?

Going back to verse 1, we see that Paul addressed his letter to

> all the saints in Christ Jesus who are in Philippi, including the overseers and deacons.

Paul mentions two groups: "the saints," meaning all believers, and the "overseers and deacons," who made up the leadership in that local church. As to the kind of people they were, Paul gives us some insight with his commendation of their giving.

> And you yourselves also know, Philippians, that at the first preaching of the gospel, after I departed from Macedonia, no church shared with me in the matter of giving and receiving but you alone; for even in Thessalonica you sent a gift more than once for my needs. (4:15–16)

The Philippians were generous, caring people, most of whom were young in the faith. At the time Paul wrote this letter, only ten years had passed since the day he first evangelized Philippi.

### Why Was It Written?

Certainly one reason Paul wrote was to thank the Philippians for their faithful support (4:14–16). Then, too, he wrote to warn them of predatory enemies.

> Beware of the dogs, beware of the evil workers, beware of the false circumcision. . . .
>
> Brethren, join in following my example, and observe those who walk according to the pattern you have in us. For many walk, of whom I often told you, and now tell you even weeping, that they are enemies of the cross of Christ, whose end is destruction, whose god is their appetite, and whose glory is in their shame, who set their minds on earthly things. (3:2, 17–19)

Finally, Paul wrote to encourage.

> Only conduct yourselves in a manner worthy of the gospel of Christ; so that whether I come and see you or remain absent, I may hear of you that you are standing firm in one spirit, with one mind striving

together for the faith of the gospel; in no way alarmed by your opponents. (1:27–28a)

## If God Is God . . . Then Laughter Fits Life

In a way, the joy reflected in Philippians is like a gem. And with each chapter, Paul reveals a different facet of that joy. For example, in chapter 1 we will learn *there is joy in living*, even when we don't get what we want (vv. 6–7), when there are difficult circumstances (vv. 12–14), or when there are conflicts (vv. 21–26). To find joy in living, there has to be something more than good feelings and comfortable settings. And that something, Paul points out, is *someone*—Christ (v. 21)!

In chapter 2, we will learn *there is joy in serving*. It starts with the right attitude, humility (vv. 3–8); is maintained through right theology (vv. 12–13); and is encouraged by the right models, such as Christ, Timothy, and Epaphroditus (vv. 5–8, 19–23, 25–30).

In chapter 3, we will learn *there is joy in sharing*. Paul shares a warning (vv. 1–2), a testimony (vv. 3–11), a goal for living (vv. 12–16), and a command (vv. 17–21).

Last, in chapter 4 we will learn *there is joy in resting*. In one of the finest pieces ever written on contentment, Paul explains how to find a joy in resting that is not controlled by circumstances (vv. 6–7, 10–13).

## Remembering a Few Significant Principles

Embedded in these four facets of joy are four lasting principles for us to remember.

First: For living joy, I need the best model—Jesus Christ (1:21).

Second: For serving with joy, I need the right attitude—an attitude like Christ's (2:5).

Third: For sharing a life of joy, I need an eternal goal—"the upward call of God in Christ Jesus" (3:14).

Fourth: For resting in joy, I need God's peace—which comes through laying our needs before Christ (4:6–7).

Philippians really is a precious gem of joy; one that sparkles with enthusiasm and encouragement because of the light of Christ that blazes so brilliantly through it. And the same can also be true of you. Jesus Christ can make our lives a living, serving, sharing, resting gem of joy. One that would make even an otter jealous!

Where do you live?

No, I don't mean where's your home. I mean where do you live *mentally?* Where do your thoughts usually travel when there's a free moment? Do they pack up and head for the past? For many, that's exactly what happens. One moment everything is fine, and the next, their thoughts have them slumming through shameful mistakes of yesterday.

For others, the problem isn't regretting the past, it's worrying about the future. You've seen the kind, fingernails bitten down to a nub, chewing on antacid tablets, always lamenting the present with some "Yeah, but" negative about the future.

Helen Mallicoat understands what it's like to live with regret and worry. She also understands where to find joy.

> I was regretting the past
> And fearing the future . . .
> Suddenly my Lord was speaking:
> "MY NAME IS I AM." He paused.
> I waited. He continued,
>
> "WHEN YOU LIVE IN THE PAST,
>     WITH ITS MISTAKES AND REGRETS
>     IT IS HARD. I AM NOT THERE.
>         MY NAME IS NOT *I WAS.*
>
> "WHEN YOU LIVE IN THE FUTURE,
>     WITH ITS PROBLEMS AND FEARS,
>     IT IS HARD. I AM NOT THERE.
>         MY NAME IS NOT *I WILL BE.*
>
> "WHEN YOU LIVE IN THIS MOMENT,
>     IT IS *NOT* HARD.
>     I AM HERE.
>         MY NAME IS *I AM.*"[3]

What is the name of the God you serve? Is it *I Was . . . I Will Be . . .* or *I Am?*

---

3. Helen Mallicoat, "I Am," as quoted by Tim Hansel in *Holy Sweat* (Waco, Tex.: Word Books, 1987), p. 136.

My friend, let me encourage you to step away from the shame and guilt of the past, remove yourself from the fear and worry of the future, and focus your attention on the joy of the Lord—who lives in the *now*. Remember the psalmist's words:

> In Thy presence is fulness of joy;
> In Thy right hand there are pleasures forever.
> (Ps. 16:11b)

 ## *Living Insights*

Now that we have seen the overall flow of joy in Philippians, let's examine the overall flow of joy in our own lives. On a scale of 1 to 10—with 1 meaning "no fizz"; 5, "bubbles occasionally"; and 10, "pops the cork"—rate yourself by circling the number that best describes the level of joy you display in that particular area.

| | | | | | | | | | | |
|---|---|---|---|---|---|---|---|---|---|---|
| Joy in living: | 1 | 2 | 3 | 4 | 5 | 6 | 7 | 8 | 9 | 10 |
| Joy in serving: | 1 | 2 | 3 | 4 | 5 | 6 | 7 | 8 | 9 | 10 |
| Joy in sharing: | 1 | 2 | 3 | 4 | 5 | 6 | 7 | 8 | 9 | 10 |
| Joy in resting: | 1 | 2 | 3 | 4 | 5 | 6 | 7 | 8 | 9 | 10 |

Of the four types of joy, do any of them pop your cork?

_____

Which one is a flat "no fizz"?

_____

For the course of this study, why don't you make it a goal to learn how to uncork the joy of the Lord you've bottled up. You may have some rare, effervescent joy coming your way!

# PHILIPPIANS: A LETTER THAT MAKES YOU SMILE

**Date:** Around A.D. 62
**Key Words:** "Rejoice," "Christ," "mind," "all"
**Key Verse:** 1:21
**Tone:** Warm, encouraging, affirming

**Uniqueness:**
- No major problem passages
- The word *joy* is found in each chapter
- Not one quotation from the Old Testament
- Christ mentioned over forty times
- Most positive of all Paul's letters, yet written while he was chained to a Roman guard

There is . . . .

|  | Joy in **Living** | Joy in **Serving** | Joy in **Sharing** | Joy in **Resting** |
|---|---|---|---|---|
|  | • when we don't get what we want<br>• in spite of circumstances<br>• even with conflicts | • starts with right attitude<br>• maintained through right theology<br>• encouraged by right models | • a warning<br>• a testimony<br>• a goal<br>• a command | • knees<br>• mind<br>• action<br>• faith |
|  | Chapter 1 | Chapter 2 | Chapter 3 | Chapter 4 |
| **Christ** | . . . My Life | . . . My Model | . . . My Goal | . . . My Contentment |
| **Spirit** | His Provision (1:19) | His Fellowship (2:1) | His Worship (1:19) | His Peace (4:7) |
| **Positive Reaction** | To Difficulty:<br>"Now I want you to know brethren, that my circumstances have turned out for the greater progress of the gospel." (1:12) | To Others:<br>"Do all things without grumbling or disputing." (2:14) | To the Past:<br>". . . forgetting what lies behind and reaching forward to what lies ahead, I press on toward the goal for the prize of the upward call of God in Christ Jesus." (3:13–14) | To the Unchangeables:<br>"Not that I speak from want: for I have learned to be content in whatever circumstances I am" (4:11) |

Chapter 2

# SET YOUR SAILS FOR JOY
*Philippians 1:1–11*

I t's been said that if you were to trace Paul's journeys in the first
century, it would be like tracking the path of a wounded deer
running from a hunter, leaving one bloody trail after another. In
2 Corinthians 11, Paul did a little tracing himself over some of those
bloodstained trails.

> Five times I received from the Jews thirty-nine lashes.
> Three times I was beaten with rods, once I was stoned,
> three times I was shipwrecked, a night and a day I
> have spent in the deep. I have been on frequent jour-
> neys, in dangers from rivers, dangers from robbers,
> dangers from my countrymen, dangers from the Gen-
> tiles, dangers in the city, dangers in the wilderness,
> dangers on the sea, dangers among false brethren; I
> have been in labor and hardship, through many sleep-
> less nights, in hunger and thirst, often without food,
> in cold and exposure. Apart from such external things,
> there is the daily pressure upon me of concern for
> all the churches. (vv. 24–28)

Physically, Paul must have been a wreck. Everywhere he traveled
he carried on his body a shocking diary of scars that visibly testified
to the murderous hatred and hardships he had endured.

All that suffering, yet Paul still spoke of joy in his letter to the
church at Philippi. How? How could this man, writing as a prisoner
from Rome, press out a deep, rich joy from such bitter circumstances, past and present? Because he was *confident* that God was
at work, that God was in control, and that God allowed all things
to occur for one ultimate purpose—His greater glory!

Paul understood that joy doesn't depend upon circumstances,
people, or possessions. It is an *attitude* that's determined by confidence in God. And regardless of how difficult the path, how bloody
the trail, Paul continually chose to put his confidence in God. Or, as
poet Ella Wheeler Wilcox might have said, Paul set his sails for joy.

> One ship drives east and another drives west
> With the selfsame winds that blow.

'Tis the set of the sails
And not the gales
Which tells us the way to go.[1]

Paul's confidence in God guided him like an inner compass, always keeping him on joy's course regardless of the gales that blew. Do you have that same inner confidence guiding you? Come, let Paul teach you to put your confidence in God and set your sails for joy!

## A Small but Powerful Letter

In the first century, it was customary for the author of a letter to greet his or her readers in the introduction and wish them well, which is exactly what Paul does. He extends a greeting to the Philippians in verses 1–2 of chapter 1, offers up joyful thanksgiving for them in verses 3–8, and finally prays for them in verses 9–11.

When the Philippians broke the seal on this letter, the first word they read was their beloved apostle's name, Paul (v. 1). He was to those first-century Philippians what Luther was to the German Christians in the sixteenth century, what Lincoln was to the black Americans in the nineteenth century, what Churchill was to the British in the twentieth century—a respected leader, teacher, and friend.

Alongside Paul's name was another they immediately recognized, Timothy. Who could forget young Timothy? He had been with Paul when he first came to Philippi. He was there when Paul preached at the place of prayer by the river. He was there when Paul cast the spirit of divination out of the slave girl. And he had been there to comfort the foundling church in Philippi when Paul and Silas were hauled off by the authorities to be beaten and imprisoned.

Paul mentions Timothy not because he coauthored the letter, but because Timothy was known and loved by the Philippians, and because Paul hoped to send this trusted disciple to visit them again soon (see 2:19–23).

### From Servants to Saints

In the eyes of the Philippians, Paul and Timothy were probably greater-than-life heroes. In Paul's eyes, however, he and Timothy are something quite different, merely "bond-servants of Christ Jesus" (1:1a).

---

1. Ella Wheeler Wilcox, "The Winds of Fate," in *The Best Loved Poems of the American People*, comp. Hazel Felleman (Garden City, N.Y.: Doubleday and Co., 1936), p. 364, first stanza.

The Greek term Paul uses to describe himself and Timothy is *doulos,* which means:

> One bound to another . . . by the bands of a con-
> straining love. . . . One who is in a relation to an-
> other which only death can break. . . . One whose
> will is swallowed up in the . . . sweet will of God.
> . . . One who serves another even to the disregard
> of his own interests.[2]

All that and more is in Paul's mind when he refers to their being bond servants of the Savior. Not celebrities, not prima donnas to be handled with kid gloves—slaves! Paul was not only confident in God, he was also confident of his role as a bond servant, which was another reason for his joy.

Next, Paul identifies those he writes:

> To all the saints in Christ Jesus who are in Philippi,
> including the overseers and deacons. (v. 1b)

From the youngest to the oldest, the immature to the mature, the followers to the leaders, Paul calls them by the one name that fits them all—*saints.* The title means "to set apart." The Philippian believers were living, vibrant witnesses set apart from the slavery of sin to a life of holiness and service to God.

### Both Grace and Peace

Paul then commends two blessings to the saints in Philippi using the traditional greeting phrases of the Greeks and the Hebrews:

> Grace to you and peace from God our Father and
> the Lord Jesus Christ. (v. 2)

Greek letters always began with *charis—grace*—which simply meant "joy" or "pleasure." And the Hebrew word for *peace, eirēnē,* was the usual greeting shared among the Jews. Paul, however, takes both these common words and endows them with richer, deeper definitions that are uniquely Christian. The grace Paul extends to the Philippians means God's free, unmerited favor toward all unde-serving sinners. This grace is something that comes *to us.* Peace, on the other hand, is something that transpires *in us* as a result of receiving God's grace.

2. Kenneth S. Wuest, *Wuest's Word Studies from the Greek New Testament* (Grand Rapids, Mich.: William B. Eerdmans Publishing Co., 1973), vol. 2, pp. 26–27.

In its earliest form, *peace* meant "to bind together." It communicated the idea of being bound so closely together with someone or something that a harmony developed between the two. That's why Isaiah could write,

"The steadfast of mind Thou wilt keep in perfect
      peace,
Because he trusts in Thee." (26:3)

Paul experienced that kind of peace. His confidence in God was steadfast, his sails were set for joy, and he had every intention of encouraging the Philippians to sail with him!

## Joyful Thanksgiving

After his gracious greeting, Paul tells the Philippians what a source of joy and thanksgiving they are in his life. From his words, we can learn much about his relationship with these first-century believers.

### Happy Memories

I thank my God in all my remembrance of you,
always offering prayer with joy in my every prayer
for you all. (Phil. 1:3–4)

The memories that fill Paul's mind from his stay in Philippi ten years earlier are all happy ones. He harbors no regrets, no ill feelings, no unresolved conflicts; just a joy that christens his every memory and makes his every prayer a delight.

Paul then gives the reason for his thanksgiving and joy in verse 5:

In view of your participation in the gospel from the
first day until now.

The church at Philippi wasn't one of those that started out hot only to turn cold as soon as the Apostle left. They were consistent, alive, and actively participating in the gospel on their own.

### Firm Confidence

In addition to his happy memories, Paul has a firm confidence in the Philippians' spiritual growth.

For I am confident of this very thing, that He who
began a good work in you will perfect it until the
day of Christ Jesus. (v. 6)

Look again at that verse, carefully. Can you see the three reasons why Paul was confident enough to be joyful? The Apostle was absolutely convinced that God was at work in the church at Philippi, that He was in full control of that church, and that everything about that church followed a plan for His glory.

Perhaps the easiest way to summarize Paul's reasons for joy is with the two words *began* and *perfect*. The word for *perfect* that Paul uses here shares the same root term used by the disciple John when he recorded Jesus' final words on the cross, "It is *finished!*" (see John 19:30, emphasis added). The One who had begun the work would stay at it, perfect it, finish it. That's what gave Paul confidence.

> For it is only right for me to feel this way about you
> all, because I have you in my heart, since both in
> my imprisonment and in the defense and confirma-
> tion of the gospel, you all are partakers of grace with
> me. (Phil. 1:7)

Far from being the hard-bitten, distant apostle some accuse him of being, Paul could be very vulnerable at times, as he is here. In Greek, this sentence is grammatically ambiguous—we can't tell whether Paul meant "because I have you in my heart" or "because you have me in your heart." Perhaps Paul meant for this ambiguity to indicate the truth of both. Either way, verse 8 takes out all the uncertainties and makes Paul's feelings about the Philippians perfectly clear.

### Warm Affection

Paul not only had great confidence in the Philippians, he also held a warm affection for them.

> For God is my witness, how I long for you all with
> the affection of Christ Jesus. (v. 8)

The Greek word used here for *affection* is *splagchnon*, meaning "bowels." In the first century it was believed that the seat of our deepest emotions was in the intestines, heart, liver, and lungs. And though it may seem odd to us, to the Philippians Paul was conveying the tenderest of emotions.

## Specific Praying

Paul does more than simply long for his friends, however. He also prays for them.

And this I pray, that your love may abound still more and more in real knowledge and all discernment, so that you may approve the things that are excellent, in order to be sincere and blameless until the day of Christ; having been filled with the fruit of righteousness which comes through Jesus Christ, to the glory and praise of God. (vv. 9–11)

### Abounding Love

Uppermost on Paul's heart is a desire to see the Philippians' love grow. Like a river, however, their love needed banks to keep it within its proper boundaries. Otherwise they might pour out their love on the wrong things (compare 1 John 2:15–17).

To guide their love, Paul prays for two things: real knowledge and "all discernment." Those are the banks. Full and complete knowledge on one side and a keen awareness of right and wrong on the other.

### Keen Discernment

If you've ever seen a region that's been flooded, you know the desolation those rampaging waters can wreak. In a similar way, unchecked love can cause its own kind of damage and desolation. Without discernment, love blindly donates to whatever cause comes to the door. With it, love learns to spot the phony, the wrong, the evil —and, as Paul says, "approve the things that are excellent" (v. 10).

According to one commentator, the term *approve* means "to sift or test a certain thing and thus to recognize its worth and put their stamp of approval upon it."[3] When that happens, we've returned again to the key that unlocks joy—confidence.

## Practical Application

From the second stanza of her poem "The Winds of Fate," Ella Wheeler Wilcox hails one last reminder about setting our sails for joy.

> Like the winds of the sea are the ways of fate,
> As we voyage along through life:
> 'Tis the set of a soul
> That decides its goal,
> And not the calm or the strife.[4]

3. Wuest, *Wuest's Word Studies*, p. 37.
4. Wilcox, "The Winds of Fate," in *Best Loved Poems*, p. 364, second stanza.

As you prepare to launch into the calm and strife of your day, set the course of your soul according to these three guiding principles from Paul: First, *confidence brings joy when you focus on the things for which you're thankful* (v. 3). Second, *confidence brings joy when you let God be God* (v. 6). And third, *confidence brings joy when you keep love within its proper limits* (v. 9).

## Living Insights                                                    STUDY ONE

Giving thanks is becoming a lost art. In our affluent Western society, we're so used to getting what we want when we want it that we take a lot of things for granted—including God. As a result, we often forfeit our joy because we've forgotten how to be truly thankful.

When was the last time you knelt before God to offer up thanksgiving—and nothing else? When was the last time you heard someone else do this? It's easy to understand why the world doesn't see much joy reflected in Christianity today. We've quit practicing the art of thanksgiving, and without it, joy will remain a very scarce commodity.

Take a moment to read the exhortations to give thanks in the following passages: 1 Thessalonians 5:18; Ephesians 5:4, 15–20; Philippians 4:6.

Now take a look at a couple of examples of thanksgiving: Exodus 15:1–21 and Psalm 136. Those people really knew how to give thanks, didn't they?

Are you interested in becoming an apprentice in the art of thanksgiving? Spend a little more time in the Psalms and begin personalizing their praise. Psalms 103 through 106 are good ones to start with. Or, if you like, use the space provided to write your own psalm of thanksgiving to God.

_____

_____

_____

_____

_____

_____

_____

## 🍇 _Living Insights_

Here's a practical suggestion to help you cultivate the art of thanksgiving in your family.

Right along with those cherished photo albums that chronicle the important events and people in your lives, why not keep a scrapbook of God's blessings? Have each member of the family contribute once a month, once every six months, or whenever by writing down the things they feel especially thankful for. Then at Thanksgiving, make it a tradition to have everyone read what they've written and give thanks together as a family (Pss. 105:1–5; 77:11–15; 1 Chron. 16:1–36).[5]

---

5. Living Insights, Studies One and Two, are taken from Charles R. Swindoll, _Living Above the Level of Mediocrity_ (Dallas, Tex.: Word Publishing, 1989), pp. 294–95.

## Chapter 3

# WHAT A WAY TO LIVE!

*Philippians 1:12–21*

We hold these truths to be self-evident,
that all men are created equal,
that they are endowed by their Creator
with certain unalienable Rights,
that among these are Life,
Liberty and the pursuit of Happiness.[1]

If it is our unalienable right to pursue happiness, why have so few of us found it? Why, after two hundred years of progress, haven't we made more headway in capturing this elusive prize?

The answer lies in that one word *pursuit.* To pursue something suggests that it's outside of us, that it's somewhere "out there" needing to be discovered or caught. But happiness doesn't come from without; it comes from within. It is not dependent on outward circumstances, but on an inner mind-set. It's a choice, not a pursuit.

Holocaust survivor Viktor Frankl wrote,

> Everything can be taken from a man but one thing: the last of the human freedoms—to choose one's attitude in any given set of circumstances, to choose one's own way.[2]

If we pursue happiness instead of choosing joy, we will become, as Frankl put it, "plaything[s] of circumstance."[3] Our inner peace will be tossed back and forth according to the whim of events beyond our control. But if we exercise our "right" to choose our attitude—the one basic freedom that can't be taken away from us—we can choose joy even in the midst of the cruelest circumstances.

---

1. *The New Encyclopaedia Britannica: Micropaedia*, 15th ed., see "The Declaration of Independence," vol. 10, p. 1039.

2. Viktor E. Frankl, *Man's Search for Meaning*, rev. ed. (New York, N.Y.: Simon and Schuster, Pocket Books, 1984), p. 86.

3. Frankl, *Man's Search for Meaning*, p. 87.

## Needed: A Positive Mind-Set

Many of us search desperately for circumstances that will make us happy, while others deliberately choose joy despite the ever-changing panorama of health or external pleasures or people in their lives. If contrasted, these two different approaches might look something like this:

| Negative Mind-Set | Positive Mind-Set |
|---|---|
| • Those who need certain *things* before they can be joyful. | • Those who need virtually *nothing* tangible to give them joy. |
| • Those who are dependent on *others* to provide joy. | • Those who create their *own* reasons for joy. |
| • Those who see joy as being *"out there"*—always future. | • Those who choose it *now,* making it a present reality. |

It's not enough, however, to simply say, "I choose to be joyful." To choose joy means that we set our minds on the kinds of things specifically listed in Philippians 4:8.

> Finally, brethren, whatever is true, whatever is honorable, whatever is right, whatever is pure, whatever is lovely, whatever is of good repute, if there is any excellence and if anything worthy of praise, let your mind dwell on these things.

Think of the mind as a bank that regularly receives deposits. By depositing the kinds of thoughts mentioned above, we build up and draw on a rich account that will constantly yield a high dividend called joy.

## Paul: A Classic Example of How to Live

To find proof that joy is something we choose rather than pursue, we need not look any further than the apostle Paul. Let's go back a few pages in his life and thumb through the events that led up to his letter to the Philippians.

It all began years before, when the Apostle was falsely accused of desecrating the temple in Jerusalem. He was dragged out of there by a lynch mob and was nearly beaten to death before Roman soldiers from the local garrison intervened. Thinking that he was an Egyptian renegade, the soldiers' commander ordered that Paul be bound with chains and taken to their barracks (Acts 21).

When the commander, Claudius Lysias, couldn't decide what to do with Paul, he sent him to Felix, the governor of Caesarea. When Felix couldn't decide after two years how to handle Paul's case, he left him in prison for his successor, Porcius Festus, to deal with. When Festus couldn't decide either, he tried to placate Paul's accusers by asking the Apostle to return to Jerusalem and stand trial. Knowing that this would result in his being murdered, Paul refused, claiming his right as a Roman citizen to appeal his case before Caesar (Acts 22–25).

Several months and a shipwreck later, Paul finally arrived in Rome. He had longed to come to this great city as a preacher, but he arrived instead as a prisoner. And he spent the next two years of his life under house arrest awaiting his day in court (chaps. 27–28).

Despite being a victim of false accusations, unlawful arrest, and unfair imprisonment, Paul continued exercising his unalienable right to choose joy, as we shall see in the following excerpt from his letter to the Philippians.

### Confident, Even Though a Victim

In light of the circumstances surrounding Paul's imprisonment, notice what he chooses to focus on.

> Now I want you to know, brethren, that my circumstances have turned out for the greater progress of the gospel, so that my imprisonment in the cause of Christ has become well known throughout the whole praetorian guard and to everyone else, and that most of the brethren, trusting in the Lord because of my imprisonment, have far more courage to speak the word of God without fear. (Phil. 1:12–14)

Paul sees progress being made where many would see only regress. Rather than viewing his confinement as an impediment to his preaching, he points out how his circumstances are actually assisting the spreading of the gospel. To illustrate this, Paul uses a vivid term for progress, prokopē, that depicts a group of woodcutters clearing the way through an impenetrable forest for an advancing army. In the same way, he felt that his imprisonment was clearing the way for the gospel in areas that were previously impossible to reach.

One of those areas was Rome's imperial regiment of soldiers known as the Praetorian Guard. Even though Paul lived in his own rented quarters (Acts 28:30), he was constantly chained to the wrist of a soldier (v. 16). But with each changing of the guard came a new opportunity for sharing Christ. For two years the guards heard Paul pray, preach, and dictate epistles. They listened as he conversed with others about the consequences of sin and forgiveness through Jesus Christ. And in this way, the gospel penetrated the imperial barracks.

None of this would have happened, of course, if Paul had chosen to complain to God and to his guard about his circumstances. In focusing on how the Lord was using his situation, however, he encouraged others to proclaim Christ. And that gave him something to smile about.

### Joyful, in Spite of Others

Paul rejoiced even knowing that not all those who proclaimed the gospel did so with the same guileless intent that he brought to the task.

> Some, to be sure, are preaching Christ even from envy and strife, but some also from good will; the latter do it out of love, knowing that I am appointed for the defense of the gospel; the former proclaim Christ out of selfish ambition, rather than from pure motives, thinking to cause me distress in my imprisonment. What then? Only that in every way, whether in pretense or in truth, Christ is proclaimed; and in this I rejoice, yes, and I will rejoice. (Phil. 1:15–18)

A paraphrase of verse 18 might read, "So what if some preach with wrong motives. So what if some are overly interested in themselves. So what if there are some who take unfair shots at me. What matters is this: Christ is being preached, and that thought alone intensifies my joy!"

There was a time, however, when Paul was not joyful in spite of what others preached, when he didn't simply say, "So what?" On the contrary, his advice to the Galatians was to let certain others be anathema—accursed!

> I am amazed that you are so quickly deserting Him who called you by the grace of Christ, for a different gospel; which is really not another; only

there are some who are disturbing you, and want to distort the gospel of Christ. But even though we, or an angel from heaven, should preach to you a gospel contrary to that which we have preached to you, let him be accursed. As we have said before, so I say again now, if any man is preaching to you a gospel contrary to that which you received, let him be accursed. (Gal. 1:6–9)

Why does Paul say in one letter, "Let him be accursed," and in another, "So what?" Isn't his contrasting advice of condemnation and indifference contradictory? No, and the reason is simple. In Galatians, the Apostle is denouncing those who garble the gospel of grace into a message of works. In Philippians, he's rejoicing that, despite the impure motives of some, the good news of Jesus Christ is still being proclaimed accurately. The message mattered most to Paul, not the messenger. Sure, he didn't enjoy hearing about the selfish ambition of some, but he would not let their wrong motives rob him of the joy of Jesus being preached.

### Hopeful, Regardless of Uncertainties

With the gospel spreading and people proclaiming Christ all because of his imprisonment, Paul was greatly encouraged. And this helped him continue trusting in God instead of focusing on the uncertainties of his circumstances.

For I know that this shall turn out for my deliverance through your prayers and the provision of the Spirit of Jesus Christ, according to my earnest expectation and hope, that I shall not be put to shame in anything, but that with all boldness, Christ shall even now, as always, be exalted in my body, whether by life or by death. (Phil. 1:19–20)

You won't find any self-pity in these words, because for Paul the most important thing in life wasn't his plans or his personal comfort, it was exalting Jesus.

### Contented, Because Christ Was Central

Paul then declares the most self-evident of all truths concerning his life, the one that enabled him to endure all his difficulties with transcendent joy: "For to me, to live is Christ, and to die is gain" (v. 21).

22

The Living Bible paraphrases it like this: "For to me, living means opportunities for Christ, and dying—well, that's better yet!"

Phillips translates it, "For living to me means simply 'Christ,' and if I die I should merely gain more of him."

The Good News Bible reads, "For what is life? To me, it is Christ. Death, then, will bring more."

If Paul had lived for anything but Jesus, his statement as well as his life would have ended with a loss instead of a gain. The truth of this becomes evident in these altered versions of that same verse.

- "For to me, to live is money, and to die is to leave it all behind."

- "For to me, to live is fame, and to die is to be forgotten."

- "For to me, to live is power, and to die is to lose it all."

- "For to me, to live is possessions, and to die is to take none of them with me."

The "pursuit of happiness," according to Paul, is the pursuit of Christ; that's the secret of joy—cultivating a Christ-centered mindset. He told the Colossians as much when he wrote:

> If then you have been raised up with Christ, keep seeking the things above, where Christ is, seated at the right hand of God. *Set your mind on the things above*, not on the things that are on earth. For you have died and your life is hidden with Christ in God. When Christ, who is our life, is revealed, then you also will be revealed with Him in glory. (Col. 3:1–4, emphasis added)

## And You? Three Things to Remember

The day we quit pursuing happiness and choose to follow Christ will be the day we discover the same joy that replaced Paul's anxieties and fears with a calm contentment and peace. We'll also discover that Jesus will impact our lives in the same three areas that Paul described in our lesson today—circumstances, relationships, and the future.

*When Christ is central, He broadens the dimensions of our circumstances.* Jesus wasn't bound by Paul's chains, nor is He confined by our limitations. In every circumstance, He is "able to do exceeding abundantly beyond all that we ask or think" (Eph. 3:20a). He can turn a loss into a gain, a weakness into a strength, a prison into a place of proclamation. And that gives us confidence.

*When Christ is central, He delivers us from a preoccupation with others.* Paul's joy wasn't dependent on others; he didn't need anyone's approval—he had Christ, and His approval was all that mattered. When we put Jesus above all others, that brings us joy.

*When Christ is central, He calms our fears regarding ourselves and our future.* When the person of Christ is in full focus, at the center of our hearts and minds, we find contentment instead of insecurity, peace instead of anxiety, joy instead of fear. And that instills in us a hope for the future.

## Living Insights STUDY ONE

How would you define joy and happiness? Without using a dictionary, write down your own definition in the space provided. Try to avoid writing what you think is right, and put down instead what you were brought up to believe.

Joy _____

_____

Happiness _____

_____

Many of us have been raised to believe that joy and happiness mean the same thing. But, as Tim Hansel points out in his book *Holy Sweat,* they are actually quite different.

> But what is joy? Is it the same as happiness? Not really. Joy is oftentimes a misunderstood concept. We get the picture of someone "jumping for joy"— "crying for joy"—"dancing for joy." But joy is something quite different.
> 1. *Joy is not the same as happiness.*
> Happiness depends on circumstances. In fact, the word itself comes from the same root word as *happening.* It means that something good has happened to you. For example, if I get a new shirt, I'm

happy. If I eat a good meal, I'm happy. If I paid off my car, I'd be happy. In fact, I'd probably be *really* happy.

There's certainly nothing wrong with that. I encourage people to get as much happiness as they can—but we should realize that happiness is always based on circumstances, on "happenings."

Happiness is not the same as joy. Because circumstances allow happiness, they can also make happiness dissolve into thin air. Joy, on the other hand, defies circumstances. It can coexist with doubt, ambiguity, and pain. It is a contentedness beyond circumstances, an indestructible kind of confidence.[4]

With that difference in mind, let's take our understanding of joy a step further in the right direction. Write a new definition for it based on what we learned from Paul in our lesson.

Joy _____

_____

_____


### Living Insights

Even as Christians, many of us are still caught on the American Dream treadmill of pursuing happiness. Our minds are still programmed to think that lasting joy is out there, just waiting for us when we buy that new car or home. Honestly, does that describe you? Do you often find yourself thinking how good life would be if only you had certain things?

We spend far more time than any of us likes to admit window shopping for joy while dressed in drab attitudes. But it's true. And we've always got excuses, even though we prefer to label them "reasons," for why we're not happy. "If only I had this . . . If only he would do that . . . If only . . ."

"If only" means our eyes are on the horizon, still searching, waiting for our ship to come in so we can be joyful.

How would you like to quit waiting? How would you like to exchange those worn-out melancholy attitudes you're wearing for

4. Tim Hansel, *Holy Sweat* (Waco, Tex.: Word Books, 1987), p. 133.

joy? In his excellent book *Effective Biblical Counseling,* Dr. Larry Crabb offers this advice:

> Many of us place top priority not on becoming Christlike in the middle of our problems but on finding happiness. I want to be happy but the paradoxical truth is that I will never be happy if I am concerned primarily with becoming happy. My overriding goal must be in every circumstance to respond biblically, to put the Lord first, to seek to behave as He would want me to. The wonderful truth is that as we devote all our energies to the task of becoming what Christ wants us to be, He fills us with joy unspeakable and a peace far surpassing what the world offers. . . .
>
> Paul said it was his ambition (goal) not to become happy but to please God at every moment. What a transforming thought! When I drive my car to work and someone cuts me off, when my kids act up during church, when the dishwasher breaks—my primary responsibility is to *please God!*[5]

As Jesus said, we cannot serve two masters, for we'll always end up hating one and loving the other. "You cannot serve God and mammon" (Matt. 6:24b). Is happiness your mammon? Is pleasing God second or third or fourth to becoming happy? There's only one way to free yourself from the tyranny of "the pursuit of happiness" and find true joy, and that's by making it your goal to please God instead.

In what practical ways this week can you build up, encourage, reinforce the mind-set of pleasing Christ?

_____

_____

_____

5. Lawrence J. Crabb, Jr., *Effective Biblical Counseling* (Grand Rapids, Mich.: Zondervan Publishing House, 1977), pp. 20–21.

## Chapter 4
# LAUGHING THROUGH LIFE'S DILEMMAS
### Philippians 1:21–30

Wouldn't it be nice if making decisions became easier with age? It would be great if the more gray hairs we grew, the more black and white the issues would become; the more our vision blurred, the more clearly we could distinguish between right and wrong; the more we lost our shape, the more well-defined wisdom and foolishness would appear.

But life's not like that. We do get older, but the decisions don't get any easier. In fact, the situations we face as adults are often more grizzled and ill-defined than we are!

Dilemmas *are* like that. They're complicated, fuzzy, head-scratching predicaments that refuse to be resolved with a simplistic "this is right and that's wrong" kind of approach. Why? Because there are always advantages and disadvantages to both sides in a dilemma. No matter which side you choose, you lose something. There's no clear winner in these kinds of decisions. And that's why, to use an old expression, dilemmas put us between a rock and a hard place.

## Familiar Dilemmas, Commonly Faced

Have you ever felt the pressure and confusion of having to decide something that wasn't black and white, right or wrong? Then you've probably experienced one or more of the following three kinds of dilemmas.

### Volitional Dilemmas

Volitional dilemmas happen when we want to do two different things at the same time. For instance, a young married couple want to start a family, but they each have two more demanding years of graduate school ahead of them. Do they go ahead and have children or finish school first?

### Emotional Dilemmas

An emotional dilemma occurs when we have conflicting feelings about a difficult situation. For example, say a beloved family pet contracts a painful disease in old age. What does the family do if the vet has nothing that will cure the problem? Should they let the pet die naturally or put it to sleep?

### Geographical Dilemmas

When we desire to be in two different places at the same time, we face a geographical dilemma. Being offered a better job in a new location often precipitates this kind of difficult decision. To accept the job might mean a significant pay raise and more opportunity for advancement in the future. But it would also mean uprooting the family from familiar surroundings, close friends, and a good church. Move or stay, which would be better?

In our lesson today, we'll find the apostle Paul wrestling with a similar rock-and-a-hard-place dilemma, one that's not only geographical, but intensely emotional and volitional as well.

## Paul's Personal Dilemma

In our last lesson, remember, Paul told the Philippians that Jesus was his life, his joy, his one consuming passion. "For to me, to live is Christ, and to die is gain" (Phil. 1:21). Paul wanted Jesus to be exalted in his body in every way, "whether by life or by death" (v. 20). And death was certainly a possibility if his accusers had their way in court or in an ambush on some deserted road.

The thought of martyrdom didn't depress Paul, however. In fact, he got downright homesick thinking about being in heaven with Jesus, unshackled and free. Dying really would be a "gain" to Paul. And that's the essence of his dilemma.

> But if I am to live on in the flesh, this will mean fruitful labor for me; and I do not know which to choose. But I am hard-pressed from both directions, having the desire to depart and be with Christ, for that is very much better; yet to remain on in the flesh is more necessary for your sake. (vv. 22–24)

The Apostle's desire to join Jesus in heaven and yet, at the same time, to remain with the Philippians on earth has him between a rock and a hard place. He feels torn in two directions: "I do not know which to choose" (v. 22).

As in all dilemmas, both sides of the issue have benefits and liabilities. Let's take a brief look at what some of these were for Paul.

28

### Option 1: To Depart

*Benefit:* In Paul's mind, the gain of dying was that he would instantly be with Christ, free from the frustrations and pain of this world. No more stonings, beatings, and imprisonments. No more thorn in the flesh; no more living with constant danger, hunger, thirst, and sleepless nights of hardship. He would have unending peace instead, in a place of perfection, in the very presence of God. He would know fullness of joy and experience eternal pleasures from God's own hand (Ps. 16:11).

*Liability:* Paul knew, however, that to be with Jesus meant that he would be absent from those who needed him. The Philippians were his spiritual children, and to leave them would be like a father abandoning his family. Such a loss would surely hamper their growth. Also, he would no longer be a witness to his Roman guards day after day, nor would he reach any others for Christ through missionary journeys. The infant church, which relied on his authority and guidance, would be bereft of their great champion as well.

### Option 2: To Remain

*Benefit:* By staying, Paul knew he could continue nurturing the Philippians' growth and maturity in the Lord. This would not only give them greater security and hope for the future, it would also bring Paul much joy in their relationship. His writing ministry, too, would continue, bringing God's grace and truth to countless generations he would never see.

*Liability:* To stay obviously meant Paul would remain chained to Rome instead of going home to heaven.

As badly as Paul wants to be with Christ, he chooses to stay instead, exemplifying Christ to the Philippians by selflessly placing their needs above his own desires.

> And convinced of this, I know that I shall remain and continue with you all for your progress and joy in the faith, so that your proud confidence in me may abound in Christ Jesus through my coming to you again.[1] (Phil. 1: 25–26)

---

1. In verse 26 Paul, far from boasting about himself, is saying that his release from imprisonment and subsequent return to Philippi would cause the church there to "abound" in their "proud confidence" in Christ.

# Philippians' Spiritual Challenge

Having committed himself to remain, Paul immediately issues a challenge to ensure the Philippians' "progress and joy in the faith."

> Only conduct yourselves in a manner worthy of the gospel of Christ; so that whether I come and see you or remain absent, I may hear of you that you are standing firm in one spirit, with one mind striving together for the faith of the gospel; in no way alarmed by your opponents—which is a sign of destruction for them, but of salvation for you, and that too, from God. For to you it has been granted for Christ's sake, not only to believe in Him, but also to suffer for His sake, experiencing the same conflict which you saw in me, and now hear to be in me. (vv. 27–30)

For a closer look at what Paul means by "conduct . . . worthy of the gospel of Christ," let's contrast the positive and negative aspects of his challenge.

### Positive

The Philippians are told to stand firm in one spirit with one mind, in two different respects (v. 27b). First, among themselves Paul wants there to be a unity and harmony. And second, before others, they are to exhibit solidarity and courage in striving together for the gospel. In Greek, the word for *striving* is an athletic, blood-sweat-and-tears kind of term. The Philippians have seen Paul fight the good fight of faith by the sweat of his brow; now he exhorts them to do the same.

### Negative

Paul tells them not to be "alarmed by their opponents." The term *alarmed* literally pictures a horse shying away from the battlefield. The Philippians aren't to go out looking for trouble, but when conflicts flare up, there is no reason to be shy or hesitant. And the Apostle gives them several reasons why.

(1) They're not alone (v. 27). They are to strive *together* for the gospel. It's frightening to face opposition alone, but there's comfort in having others on your side who are also by your side.

(2) Paul gives them the subtle assurance that, ultimately, the victory is theirs (v. 28). Commentator F. F. Bruce sheds some light on this promise.

The presence of opposition, Paul assures them, shows that they are on the right path in their active gospel witness. It is a token of salvation to them, as it is a token of perdition for their opponents: "they will lose and . . . you will win" [GNB]. God is the author of the gospel: those who defend it may therefore expect deliverance and victory from him as surely as those who resist it may expect to incur his judgment. Much the same thought finds fuller expression in 2 Thessalonians 1:5–10.[2]

(3) The Philippians shouldn't be alarmed by their opponents because God has granted that His followers should suffer for His sake (v. 29). This is a painful but helpful reminder. Don't let opposition and suffering catch you off guard; rather, prepare for them by expecting it.

(4) Paul helps calm the Philippians' fears with the reminder that the conflicts they face, he has faced too (v. 30). Hope and encouragement often come in just knowing that someone else has already been through what you're currently experiencing.

## Our Personal Response

Making right decisions in the midst of a dilemma is tough. It forces us to rethink our priorities and reconsider the importance of Christ in our lives.

Have you been hard-pressed by a dilemma lately? Are you being torn in two directions by a rock-and-a-hard-place decision? Choosing the best solution won't be easy. So put on your bifocals if you need them; muster all the wisdom you can from past experience; and don't forget to keep your commitment to Christ as strong, black and white, and well-defined as Paul's: "For to me, to live is Christ, to die is gain" (v. 21).

## 🍇 *Living Insights*                                    STUDY ONE

Traditionally, when we list our priorities, we begin with God at the top and work our way down the list in order of importance. Usually it comes out looking something like this:

2. F. F. Bruce, *Philippians* (San Francisco, Calif.: Harper and Row, Publishers, 1983), p. 33.

God

Marriage

Family

Work

Etc.

As helpful as this is, there's a practical flaw. Shouldn't our priorities not only reflect that we seek God *above* all other things, but also that we seek to put Him first *in* everything?

God

God in my marriage

God in my family

God in my work

God in . . .

Sometimes I wonder if that first priority list hasn't inadvertently led many to view their relationship with God as totally separate from the rest of their lives. Too often we give God a few minutes in the morning, put Him back on the top shelf, then work our way down the bookcase of priorities without taking Him into account.

Seeking God in our quiet time each day should be what encourages us to seek Him in every other area of our lives. He should take priority in every thought we think, in every word we speak, in every relationship, in everything—period.

In the space provided, write out a list of, say, the top five priorities in your life. Next, beside each one, write down how much time you invest in each one on a weekly basis. Finally, even though there's no way to pin this down with a number, ask yourself, How well am I exalting Christ in each of these areas?[3]

| | *Priorities* | *Time* |
|---|---|---|
| 1. | _____ | _____ |
| 2. | _____ | _____ |

3. Based on Charles R. Swindoll, *Living Above the Level of Mediocrity* (Dallas, Tex.: Word Publishing, 1989), pp. 289–90.

3. _____ _____

4. _____ _____

5. _____ _____

## 🍇 *Living Insights*

Are you wrestling with a particular dilemma right now? It can be so confusing. Often we feel overwhelmed with all the issues involved and end up making important, life-changing decisions based simply on how we feel rather than on the facts.

One of the simplest ways to take much of the confusion out of a decision is by writing down the benefits and liabilities that you see connected with each alternative. Have you done that yet? Using the space provided, write down your dilemma, the alternatives, and the specific pluses and minuses as you see them.

Dilemma _____

### Alternative 1

_____

| | *Benefits* | *Liabilities* |
|---|---|---|
| 1. | _____ | _____ |
| 2. | _____ | _____ |
| 3. | _____ | _____ |
| 4. | _____ | _____ |
| 5. | _____ | _____ |

### Alternative 2

_____

| | *Benefits* | *Liabilities* |
|---|---|---|
| 1. | _____ | _____ |
| 2. | _____ | _____ |

3. _____ _____

4. _____ _____

5. _____ _____

When you've written down all that you can, show it to someone whose insight and wisdom you respect and ask for that person's help in identifying any other benefits and liabilities. Show it to the Lord too, and ask Him for wisdom, discernment, and direction. With His help and that of your friends, you'll find more comfort and guidance than you ever thought possible between a rock and hard place.

# Chapter 5

# THE HIDDEN SECRET
# OF A HAPPY LIFE

*Philippians 2:1–11*

O f all the Christlike attitudes that people exhibit in our world, rarely do any of them grab our hearts and minds like unselfishness—whether it is the selfless work of a well-known Mother Teresa or an unknown man in the water.

As disasters go, this one was terrible, but not unique, certainly not among the worst on the roster of U.S. air crashes. There was the unusual element of the bridge, of course, and the fact that the plane clipped it at a moment of high traffic, one routine thus intersecting another and disrupting both. Then, too, there was the location of the event. Washington, the city of form and regulations, turned chaotic, de-regulated, by a blast of real winter and a single slap of metal on metal. . . . And there was the aesthetic clash as well—blue-and-green Air Florida, the name a flying garden, sunk down among gray chunks in a black river. All that was worth noticing, to be sure. Still, there was nothing very special in any of it, except death, which, while always special, does not necessarily bring millions to tears or to attention. Why, then, the shock here? . . .

. . . The person most responsible for the emotional impact of the disaster is the one known at first simply as "the man in the water." (Balding, probably in his 50s, an extravagant mustache.) He was seen clinging with five other survivors to the tail section of the airplane. This man was described by Usher and Windsor [a park police helicopter team] as appearing alert and in control. Every time they lowered a lifeline and flotation ring to him, he passed it on to another of the passengers. "In a mass casualty, you'll find people like him," said Windsor. "But

35

I've never seen one with that commitment." When the helicopter came back for him, the man had gone under. His selflessness was one reason the story held national attention.[1]

## Analyzing Unselfishness

Unselfishness—we all have our own definitions to describe it, but words cannot explain the meaning as clearly and forcefully as that man's ultimate act of self-sacrifice in the icy waters of the Potomac.

> At some moment in the water he must have realized that he would not live if he continued to hand over the rope and ring to others. He *had* to know it, no matter how gradual the effect of the cold. In his judgment he had no choice. When the helicopter took off with what was to be the last survivor, he watched everything in the world move away from him, and he deliberately let it happen.[2]

That costly sacrifice powerfully portrays another. Two thousand years ago, the Son of God became flesh and dwelt among us. He came to pay the penalty for our sins, knowing that it would cost Him His life. In His judgment, however, He had no choice. When His betrayer took off and the disciples fled, He watched everything in the world move away from Him. And He deliberately let it happen. That's unselfishness; that's Christlikeness in one word.

## Examining Christlikeness

Christlikeness is also Paul's major concern in our lesson today. He wants Lydia, the Roman jailer, and the rest of the believers in Philippi to exemplify this same selfless attitude—an attitude essential to the church's unity, then and now.

### What Is Needed?

In the first two verses, Paul wants unselfishness to be expressed in a like-minded spirit of harmony.

---

1. Roger Rosenblatt, "The Man in the Water," *Time*, January 25, 1982, p. 86.
2. Rosenblatt, "The Man in the Water," p. 86.

If therefore there is any encouragement in Christ, if there is any consolation of love, if there is any fellowship of the Spirit, if any affection and compassion, make my joy complete by being of the same mind, maintaining the same love, united in spirit, intent on one purpose. (Phil. 2:1–2)

To better understand the implication of Paul's fourfold plea, reread verse 1 and change each "if there is" to "since there is." From this you'll see that Paul is actually affirming these qualities in the Philippians, not questioning them.[3]

Then note how these four positive assertions link with the four requests in verse 2.

- Since there is encouragement in Christ—be of the same mind.

- Since there is consolation of love—maintain that same love.

- Since there is fellowship of the Spirit—be united in spirit.

- Since there is affection and compassion—be intent on one purpose.

By encouraging the Philippians to be "of the same mind," is Paul saying that there's no room for individuality and disagreement in the church, that we should all think, dress, and act the same? Not at all. It's unity he's pleading for, not uniformity. And there's a big difference.

Unity comes from within; it's the result of an inner attitude. Uniformity, on the other hand, comes from without, the forced product of external pressures.

In his commentary on Philippians, Harry Ironside offers this insight as to how the church can achieve unity amidst diversity.

It is very evident that Christians will never see eye to eye on all points. We are so largely influenced by habits, by environment, by education, by the measure of intellectual and spiritual apprehension to which we have attained, that it is an impossibility

---

3. "The word 'if' is the translation of a conditional particle referring to a fulfilled condition. One could translate 'since,' or 'in view of the fact.' The four things mentioned in this verse are not hypothetical in their nature. They are facts." Kenneth S. Wuest, *Wuest's Word Studies from the Greek New Testament* (1973; reprint, Grand Rapids, Mich.: William B. Eerdmans Publishing Co., 1979), vol. 2, p. 56.

to find any number of people who look at everything from the same standpoint. How then can such be of one mind? The apostle himself explains it elsewhere when he says, "I think also that I have the mind of Christ." The "mind of Christ" is the lowly mind. And, if we are all of *this* mind, we shall walk together in love, considering one another, and seeking rather to be helpers of one another's faith, than challenging each other's convictions.[4]

The lowly mind of Christ is a selfless one. That's what is needed if there's to be any hope of unity.

### How Is It Accomplished?

Practical advice on how to integrate that Christlike attitude into everyday living is also needed if unity is ever to become more than just a nice idea. And Paul provides this kind of prudent counsel in verses 3–4.

Do nothing from selfishness or empty conceit, but with humility of mind let each of you regard one another as more important than himself; do not merely look out for your own personal interests, but also for the interests of others.

The three practical tips Paul mentions are (1) *never* let selfishness or conceit be your motive; (2) regard others as more important than yourself; and (3) don't limit your attention to your own personal interests—include others. Self-forgetfulness is what Paul is advocating, not self-hate. As Christians, when we pursue the goal of exalting Christ and putting others before ourselves, we tend to forget all the self-serving, petty differences that normally separate us.

Writing about Hitler's blitzkrieg bombing of Britain, Martyn Lloyd-Jones relates a vivid example of the kind of unity that self-forgetfulness can bring about.

How often during that last war were we told of the extraordinary scenes in air-raid shelters; how different people belonging to different classes, there, in the common need to shelter from the bombs and

4. H. A. Ironside, *Notes on Philippians*, rev. ed. (New York, N.Y.: Loizeaux Brothers, 1927), pp. 38–39.

death, forgot all the differences between them and became one. This was because in the common interest they forgot the divisions and the distinctions. . . . In periods of crises and common need all distinctions are forgotten and we suddenly become united.[5]

Hitler may have been able to destroy their homes and cities, but nothing in his arsenal could destroy their unity. As strong as that bond was, however, it was held together by the struggle to survive, to withstand the attack. When the threat passed, so did much of their unity.

So instead of waiting for external reasons to draw us together, Paul would have us initiate a lasting unity through a Christlike attitude. And who is there better to learn this from than Christ Himself?

## Christ's Life . . . Before and After

In this next section of his letter, Paul reveals Christ's humble attitude by showing us His life before, during, and after His coming to earth.

### Prior to His Incarnation

To highlight Jesus' lowliness of mind, Paul first reveals the height of glory the preexistent Savior enjoyed in heaven.

Have this attitude in yourselves which was also in Christ Jesus, who, although He existed in the form of God, did not regard equality with God a thing to be grasped. (vv. 5–6)

According to commentator Alfred Plummer, " 'In the form of God' means 'possessing the Divine attributes.' "[6] As the second member of the Godhead, Jesus is coexistent, coeternal, and coequal with God.[7] His life didn't begin in Mary's womb. The only thing that began within Mary was the *visible* manifestation of the Son of God. For the first time, God became flesh and blood.

5. D. Martyn Lloyd-Jones, *The Life of Joy: An Exposition of Philippians 1 and 2* (Grand Rapids, Mich.: Baker Book House, 1989), pp. 142–43.

6. Alfred Plummer, *A Commentary on St. Paul's Epistle to the Philippians* (London, England: Robert Scott, 1919), p. 42.

7. For further study, see also John 1:1 and Colossians 1:15–20.

Jesus didn't regard His exalted position as something to be grasped, however. Nothing within Him tempted Him to snatch or seize all the benefits of His role as absolute Sovereign over all. Why? Because of His lowliness of mind, His unselfish attitude.

In a state of absolute perfection and full control, Jesus willingly released it all for humanity.

Encompassed by angelic hosts who praised and adored Him, the Savior unselfishly came to those who cursed and crucified Him.

Surrounded by the Father's presence and fellowship, He unhesitatingly gave it all up for a lonely path of obedience to a cross.

### In His Coming

That incredible path, from heavenly Sovereign to earthly victim crucified on a cross, is next described in verses 7–8.

> But [He] emptied Himself, taking the form of a bond-servant, and being made in the likeness of men. And being found in appearance as a man, He humbled Himself by becoming obedient to the point of death, even death on a cross.

Consider the steps downward that Jesus took to share our humanity and die for our sins.

1. He emptied Himself.

2. He took the form of a bond servant.

3. He humbled Himself by becoming obedient unto death.

4. He accepted the most humiliating type of death: crucifixion.

To accomplish our salvation on a cross, Jesus first had to empty Himself. This does not mean that He gave up His deity; rather, it signifies that Christ set aside the independent use of His divine attributes and submitted Himself to the Father's will.

### Since His Departure

The Father's will mandated that Jesus descend into the lowest depths of suffering and hell for our sins. But once our debt was paid, God again lifted up His Son to a position of highest glory and honor.

> Therefore also God highly exalted Him, and bestowed on Him the name which is above every name,

that at the name of Jesus every knee should bow, of
those who are in heaven, and on earth, and under
the earth, and that every tongue should confess that
Jesus Christ is Lord, to the glory of God the Father.
(vv. 9–11)

God not only exalted Jesus to the highest position of authority,
He also bestowed on Him the name of highest significance. He
who willingly bowed to the Father's will in coming is now the
recipient of all knees bowing to Him.

Those who are in heaven will bow, which means the angelic
hosts and all the believers who have died before us. Those on earth
will bow, which includes everyone from the most bitter skeptic to
the most sincere follower. And those who are under the earth will
bow, which refers to the unsaved who have died, the demonic host,
and even Satan himself.

## The Great Question

The great question facing us today, this moment, is whether or
not we will voluntarily humble ourselves before the Lord Jesus or
wait until we're forced to do so. If we act now, we will be saved. If
we refuse to confess Jesus Christ as Lord while we're on the earth,
we will surely concede it one day under the earth. But by then it
will be too late for that declaration to change our eternal destiny.

Jesus is the lifeline the Father has lowered for our salvation.
There is no other way to be rescued from the penalty of our sins but by
Him. Don't wait, grab ahold of Him now while you have the chance.

### 🍇 Living Insights _____ STUDY ONE

As you read the following paraphrase of Philippians 2:3–4, per-
sonalize it by filling in the blanks with the names of two people
you're struggling to get along with right now.

Do nothing from selfishness or empty conceit, but

with humility of mind regard _____

as more important than yourself; do not merely look

out for your own personal interests, but also for the

interests of _____.

If you look closely, you'll notice that verse 3 touches on our underlying attitude, and verse 4 deals with the practical demonstration of that attitude. Which needs more work with regard to the two people you named—your attitude or your actions?

Use the space provided to answer this question; then spend some time brainstorming what changes need to be made.

First person's name: _____

Problem: _____

Suggested changes: _____

_____

_____

_____


Second person's name: _____

Problem: _____

Suggested changes: _____

_____

_____

_____


## Living Insights                                    STUDY TWO

> Although He existed in the form of God, [Jesus] did not regard equality with God a thing to be grasped, but emptied Himself, taking the form of a bond-servant, and being made in the likeness of men. (Phil. 2:6–7)

In emptying Himself, Jesus voluntarily set aside all the benefits of His exalted position to be born into this world a totally dependent, helpless baby. Think about that for a moment. The Sovereign of the universe helpless; deity umbilically dependent; the divine Word unable to utter one word. The Alpha and the Omega had to learn how to feed Himself, how to put His toys away and clean up His room. The Mighty God had to take naps because He got tired.

42

Why? All because Jesus selflessly took on flesh to serve, not to be served, and ultimately give His life a ransom for many (Mark 10:45).

Of what must you empty yourself to model that same servant's attitude? For that's part of our task, remember, as Paul told us:

> Have this attitude in yourselves which was also in Christ Jesus. (Phil. 2:5)

Are you grasping things that keep you from selflessly serving others? A title, perhaps, or a position? Maybe privileges, rights, or status? What about personal conveniences? Will you voluntarily set any of these aside, emptying yourself, so that you can serve others? Think through these questions in reference to your home, work, and church using the space provided.

Home _____

_____

Work _____

_____

Church _____

_____

## Chapter 6

# WHILE LAUGHING, KEEP YOUR BALANCE!

*Philippians 2:12–18*

D id you know . . .

Many people reading this page are doing so with the aid of bifocals. Inventor? *B. Franklin,* age 79.

The presses that printed this page were powered by electricity. One of the first harnessers? *B. Franklin,* age 40.

Some are reading this on the campus of one of the Ivy League universities. Founder? *B. Franklin,* age 45.

Others, in a library. Who founded the first library in America? *B. Franklin,* age 25.

Some got their copy through the U.S. Mail. Its father? *B. Franklin,* age 31.

Now, think fire. Who started the first fire department, invented the lightning rod, designed a heating stove still in use today? *B. Franklin,* ages 31, 43, 36.

Wit. Conversationalist. Economist. Philosopher. Diplomat. Favorite of the capitals of Europe. Journalist. Printer. Publisher. Linguist (spoke and wrote five languages). Advocate of paratroopers (from balloons) a century before the airplane was invented. All this until age 84. And he had exactly two years of formal schooling.[1]

Isn't that great? Incredible? Inspiring? Yes! But . . . it can be a bit disconcerting, too, as Mark Twain once quipped, "Few things are harder to put up with than the annoyance of a good example."[2]

---

1. "Advice to a (Bored) Young Man," *Newsweek,* February 13, 1967, pp. 114–15.

2. Mark Twain, as quoted in *Bartlett's Familiar Quotations,* 15th ed., rev. and enl., ed. Emily Morison Beck (Boston, Mass.: Little, Brown and Co., 1980), p. 624.

Some of you may be wondering why Twain would make such a tongue-in-cheek statement. Don't good examples help us work harder, reach higher? Yes again. But . . . they do have this one annoying problem. Good examples have no intrinsic power to enable us to achieve the same personal or professional accomplishments of others. Benjamin Franklin's successes may inspire us, but they cannot empower us. There's nothing available in them to make any of us the inventor he was.

If this is true, why, then, did Paul exhort us to follow Christ's example (Phil. 2:5)? If such a goal is impossible, doesn't that set us up for failure?

## Christ, Our Example

Some attempt to follow Christ's lofty example by faking it. They simply lip-sync the great virtues and doctrines of the Christian faith, focusing on image rather than substance. Others, perhaps most, frustrate themselves by intensifying their efforts and trying harder to do life exactly as Christ did.

It takes more, though, than perspiration and performance to follow Christ's example. It takes power—from the inside. And that is what separates Christ's example from all others. He can enable us to be like Him. How? Through the Holy Spirit who lives inside His followers. By His strength we can learn to keep our balance as we walk in Jesus' footsteps.

## Life, Our Challenge

In today's lesson, Paul touches on three challenging areas of our lives that need to be kept in balance through Christ's strength.

### Balancing Purpose and Power

The first challenge has to do with the believer's obedience to God.

> So then, my beloved, just as you have always obeyed, not as in my presence only, but now much more in my absence, work out your salvation with fear and trembling; for it is God who is at work in you, both to will and to work for His good pleasure. (Phil. 2:12–13)

"Work out your salvation"? Is Paul urging the Philippians to work hard to earn their salvation? Not at all—remember, he's addressing people who are believers already (see 1:1, 6, 12). What he is doing is exhorting his readers to build on the gift of eternal life that God has already given them. How? By walking in obedience, just as Christ, their example, did (2:8). And as they *work out* their salvation in this way, God will *work in* them, giving them the power to accomplish His will. That's balance. And out of that mix of personal obedience and divine empowerment the ultimate purpose of His "good pleasure" is achieved.

### Balancing Attitude and Action

Paul weighs out a second important balance, placing attitude on one side of the scale (v. 14) and action on the other (v. 15).

> Do all things without grumbling or disputing; that you may prove yourselves to be blameless and innocent, children of God above reproach in the midst of a crooked and perverse generation, among whom you appear as lights in the world. (vv. 14–15)

Paul warns against a bad attitude, which can reveal itself in two ways: "grumbling," which means low-toned, discontented mutterings; and "disputing," which means complaining and arguing with others, stirring up doubt and suspicions.[3] All of these are things Jesus never did!

What Christ did do, something this passage says that we're to imitate, was to take action on His convictions—to prove His character in a sin-filled world. Verse 15 outlines the qualities we need to emulate if we want to be like Christ.

First, we're to be *blameless.* The word in Greek points to a purity of life that is undeniable and inescapable, a character that's free from defect. Second, we're to exemplify *innocence.* Here the Greek word gives the idea of "*unmixed, unadulterated.* It is used, for instance, of wine or milk which is not mixed with water and of metal which has no alloy in it."[4] A simple yet profound definition would be "inexperienced in evil." Third, we must be *above reproach.* This means free of blemish, faultless. It was the term used of the animals sacrificed on altars. As William Barclay says, "The Christian life

---

3. In Greek, the word for *grumbling* is *gongusmon.* It even sounds like its meaning! Kenneth S. Wuest, *Wuest's Word Studies from the Greek New Testament* (1973; reprint, Grand Rapids, Mich.: William B. Eerdmans Publishing Co., 1979), vol. 2, p. 75.

4. William Barclay, *The Letters to the Philippians, Colossians, and Thessalonians,* rev. ed., The Daily Study Bible Series (Philadelphia, Pa.: Westminster Press, 1975), pp. 43–44.

must be such that it can be offered like an umblemished sacrifice to God."[5] And finally, we're to appear *as lights* that stand out like stars in the midst of a dark world.

God's goal for His children is not that we retreat from this world into secluded communities of spiritual light. Nor is it His desire that we blend into the world so much that we darken our witness. The balance lies in boldly reflecting Christ's light wherever we find ourselves (see also Matt. 5:14–16).

Those of us who burn up our energy grumbling and disputing will have little left over to shine as lights. But those who exemplify these four radiant qualities will penetrate the world's dark night and become beacons of salvation.

### Balancing Seriousness and Joy

The third area where Christ's strength is needed for balance touches on a personal fear of Paul's.

> Holding fast the word of life, so that in the day of Christ I may have cause to glory because I did not run in vain nor toil in vain. (Phil. 2:16)

Few things caused the Apostle more turmoil than the grim prospect of reviewing his life and feeling it was all a wasted effort (see also 1 Cor. 9:24–27). He expresses this apprehension by using the dual image of an athlete—"run in vain"—and a worker—"toil in vain." The Apostle's concern is that he not be like the runner whose endless hours of training didn't achieve anything, or like the laborer whose exhausting work was for nothing.

Instead, Paul prays that his life will contribute to the Philippians' ongoing sacrifice of service to God, even if it results in his death.

> But even if I am being poured out as a drink offering upon the sacrifice and service of your faith, I rejoice and share my joy with you all. (Phil. 2:17)

In his commentary on Philippians, F. F. Bruce helps us understand the meaning behind Paul's image of a first-century "drink offering."

> The life and service of Christians could be described as a sacrifice. Paul urges the Roman Christians to present themselves "as a living sacrifice to

5. Barclay, *Letters to the Philippians, Colossians, and Thessalonians*, p. 44.

God, dedicated to his service and pleasing to him" (Rom. 12:1). The Philippians' monetary gift to Paul is compared to "a sweet-smelling offering to God, a sacrifice which is acceptable and pleasing to him" (Phil. 4:18). If, then, their life of "faith" is offered as a sacrifice to God, can anything be added to complete its acceptance? When a sacrifice, such as a burnt offering with its accompanying cereal offering, was presented in the temple at Jerusalem, a drink-offering or libation of wine or olive oil might be poured over it or beside it. This was added last, and completed the sacrifice. If "my life's blood is to be poured out," says Paul, let it be poured out as a libation "on the sacrifice that your faith offers to God."[6]

In the midst of these serious concerns, Paul still balances his words with a plea for joy.

And you too, I urge you, rejoice in the same way and share your joy with me. (v. 18)

In what "way," exactly, was Paul rejoicing?

Paul was perfectly willing to make his life a sacrifice to God; and, if that happened, to him it would be all joy, and he calls on them not to mourn at the prospect but rather to rejoice. To him every call to sacrifice and to toil was a call to his love for Christ, and therefore he met it not with regret and complaint but with joy.[7]

One of life's pleasures is meeting godly people like Paul who enjoy living, who can be involved in the most serious of earthly tasks, yet maintain a sense of humor, a ready smile, and a contagious joy.

## Self, Our Battle

Even with Christ's example and power, balancing our lives won't be easy because of one major problem—self. Inside each of us is a

6. F. F. Bruce, *Philippians* (San Francisco, Calif.: Harper and Row, Publishers, 1983), p. 63.

7. Barclay, *Letters to the Philippians, Colossians, and Thessalonians*, p. 46.

rebellious nature that will do everything it can to upset our Christ-like equilibrium. It will grouse, dispute, pout, shout, do whatever it takes to convince us that we can live like Christ by trusting in our own power. But that always leads to a fall.

> Pride goes before destruction,
> And a haughty spirit before stumbling.
> (Prov. 16:18)

Here are two hints to remember as you balance your walk with Christ. First: *Control self's urges to take the credit.* Like Paul, make it your goal to exalt Christ, not self, in everything. Granted, that won't be easy, but through God's power our hearts and minds can learn to love Him more than ourselves. Second: *Conquer its tendency to take charge.* Again, this won't be easy. Expect a battle—a long one—because self will never let up in its effort to take control away from Christ. All the more reason we must never let up in our daily dependence on Him.

### *Living Insights* STUDY ONE

Have you been stealing silverware again? Now don't get huffy and deny it. You went over to your friend's house last night and shamelessly pocketed their new set of Oneida knives, forks, and spoons, didn't you?

Still pleading innocent? I didn't want to have to do this, but you leave me no choice. Julia Seton, would you share what you told us about grumbling and silverware?

> We have no more right to put our discordant states of mind into the lives of those around us and rob them of their sunshine and brightness than we have to enter their houses and steal their silverware.[8]

Now look in your pockets and see what's there. Surprise! Now how did all that silverware get there? I'll tell you, the same way that set of Gorham flatware got in my pocket—by grumbling.

We all do it . . . grumble, that is. We step into our friends' homes, offices, or Bible studies and steal their joy blind with all

---

8. Julia Seton, as quoted in *Quote Unquote*, Lloyd Cory comp. (Wheaton, Ill.: SP Publications, Victor Books, 1977), p. 67.

kinds of grousing and complaining. We're not sharing burdens and seeking counsel; grumblers don't like disclosing their faults and seeking help with their problems. We just want to utter a few discontented mutterings, pick up some silverware, and leave.

Do you know someone like this? Can you believe that person? Negative, negative, negative. Doesn't ever return a favor, talks behind everybody's back, and did you know . . . oops, there we go, grumbling.

Are you having trouble keeping grumbling out of your day-to-day conversations? If so, take a minute to memorize the following passage.

> Let no unwholesome word proceed from your mouth, but only such a word as is good for edification according to the need of the moment, that it may give grace to those who hear. (Eph. 4:29)

After memorizing this verse, write it out on a three-by-five card and place it where it can be a visible reminder to you wherever you tend to grumble the most—such as on your desk at work, near the phone, or by the coffee machine.

## 🍇 Living Insights

Once God miraculously freed Israel from slavery to Egypt, the people packed their possessions and began an epic journey to the Promised Land. Everybody was hilariously happy—until they saw the Egyptian army charging after them. Then they did some world-class grumbling. Read Exodus 14:5–14.

God graciously saved His grouchy followers by drowning Pharaoh's forces, and once again the children of Israel kicked up their heels for joy (14:15–15:21). Three days later, however, they dug those same heels in like stubborn mules to whine and complain about something else. Read Exodus 15:22–16:12.

You would think those people would have learned to trust God and stop grumbling, but as you read on, you'll see they didn't—and some tragic consequences followed. Read Exodus 17:1–7 and Numbers 14 and 16.

Reflecting on the passages you've read, use the space provided to write down your own description of a grumbler.

---

---

It's easy to be hard on the Israelites for all the times they grumbled, but ask yourself this question: When my back is against the wall because of difficult circumstances, do I humbly put my trust in God or do I grumble? "Why did you let this happen, God? Why haven't You lifted this burden? Haven't I been faithful? You owe me; all this time I've helped others, been good, and now this is how You treat me?"

Any of that sound familiar? Does your attitude toward God fit your description of a grumbler? If so, take some time now to confess and focus on God's faithful care.

## Prayer
(Use the space below to list any grumblings
that need confessing.)

_____

_____

_____

_____

_____

## Chapter 7

# FRIENDS MAKE LIFE MORE FUN

*Philippians 2:19–30*

H istory," according to Scottish essayist Thomas Carlyle, "is the essence of innumerable biographies." Or as Ralph Waldo Emerson put it, "There is properly no history; only biography."[1]

People. They are what history revolves around—not events, trends, or technical data. Flesh and blood, the kind that comes in endless snowflake varieties, is this world's most important commodity. And the most valuable, too. For people are why God sent His Son to die on a cross, and it is for people that He will one day return.

## Significant People in God's Plan

Let's go a step further and consider two more reasons why people are significant to God.

### Simple Reasons Why

First, people are eternal. No one dies and simply dissolves into oblivion. We have eternal souls whose destinations are determined by our response to the gospel of Jesus Christ. Second, we're significant because God normally accomplishes His work through people. What He could perfectly perform Himself in an instant, He has chosen, instead, to do through imperfect people over time. He could easily spread food before the hungry or pop in an angel to comfort the sick, but He intends us to be that angel and do those things.

### A General Survey of Whom

That God has chosen to work through people becomes all the more clear when you follow the history recorded in the Scriptures. Let your mind begin with Adam and Eve, Noah, Abraham, Isaac, Jacob, and his twelve sons—all in the book of Genesis. Then trace the trails of Moses, Joshua, Samson, Ruth, David, Solomon, and the whole kingly line of Israel. Follow the prophets Elijah, Elisha,

1. *The Macmillan Dictionary of Quotations* (Norwalk, Conn.: Easton Press, 1989), p. 72.

Isaiah, Jeremiah, Jonah, and the rest, and you will have reached the New Testament, where you'll encounter Mary and Joseph, John the Baptizer, and finally Jesus.

Even the Lord Jesus, when He became human, called twelve disciples to work, talk, and share His life with Him. His church was established by His friend Peter; and it matured and grew through Paul, James, and John. Just a glance at the names of the books and letters of the New Testament shows the significance of individuals and groups of people.

One of these letters in particular, named after its Hebrew recipients, further highlights God's work through people. In Hebrews 11, the author lists so many names of common men and women with uncommon faith that he runs out of space! He says that time would fail him if he were to tell of all the saints and their deeds and faith—saints "of whom the world was not worthy" (v. 38a).

Two such men whom God used in the apostle Paul's life were Timothy and Epaphroditus. Together, they encouraged Paul's heroic faith, accomplishments, and endurance while he was imprisoned in Rome. We'll meet these friends in today's passage of the Apostle's letter to the Philippians. For they are friends worth knowing—the kind of close companions that enrich life with the joy they bring.

## Special Friends in Paul's Life

It's easy to forget that even a tireless missionary like Paul needed friends. We tend to think of him as a loner, the John Wayne of the apostles. In reality, though, Paul was supported by a strong circle of friends. People like Barnabas and Silas, who were his traveling companions on several journeys; Priscilla and Aquila, whose home and tent-making business he shared; and countless others who worked with him, witnessed alongside him, even wrote for him when his eyesight began to fail.

In all his writings, however, the one friend Paul mentions more than any other is Timothy. He was the Apostle's closest companion.

### A "Son" Named Timothy

Timothy was a native of either Lystra or Derbe, cities in southern Asia Minor known today as Turkey. He came from a mixed marriage of a Jewish mother and a Greek father. Culturally, it appears that the Greek influence of the father dominated the home, since Timothy was not circumcised (Acts 16:3). Spiritually, however, Timothy was raised in the Jewish faith of his mother and grandmother, Eunice and Lois (see 2 Tim. 1:5; 3:14–15). And it was apparently the apostle Paul who led Timothy to Christ, which explains why he refers to him in 1 Corinthians 4:17 as "my beloved and faithful child in the Lord."

Timothy joined Paul on his journeys (Acts 16:1–3), and followed him to Philippi, Thessalonica, Berea, Corinth, Ephesus, and even all the way to imprisonment in Rome. So it is no surprise that, when the Apostle needed someone to return to Philippi in his place, Paul chose his best friend, Timothy, the one companion whom the Philippians already knew and loved.

> But I hope in the Lord Jesus to send Timothy to you shortly, so that I also may be encouraged when I learn of your condition. For I have no one else of kindred spirit who will genuinely be concerned for your welfare. For they all seek after their own interests, not those of Christ Jesus. But you know of his proven worth that he served with me in the furtherance of the gospel like a child serving his father. Therefore I hope to send him immediately, as soon as I see how things go with me; and I trust in the Lord that I myself also shall be coming shortly. (Phil. 2:19–24)

Paul commends Timothy to the Philippians for three reasons. First, *Timothy was a "kindred spirit"* (v. 20a). The Greek term for that descriptive phrase is actually made up of two terms: *isos*, meaning "equal," and *psuchē*, which means "soul." Combined, *isopsuchos* stands for "same-souled." Paul and Timothy were like-minded. They understood one another on a deeper level—something many people rarely experience. That doesn't mean they never disagreed, just that their hearts were linked. Their souls were knit together like Jonathan's and David's (see 1 Sam. 18:1; 20:17).

Second, *Timothy had a genuine concern* (Phil. 2:20b–21). Opening a window into Timothy's inner character, Paul shows us that he was a man of compassion who genuinely cared for others— someone who modeled the very Christlike attitude Paul had just written about (vv. 3–5). No wonder Paul and Timothy were so close. Their interest in others was real, authentic. This trait appears to have been just as rare then as it is today, since Paul wrote in verse 21, "For they all seek after their own interests, not those of Christ Jesus."

54

Third, *Timothy had a servant's heart* (vv. 22–24). "Like a child serving his father," Timothy served with Paul. He understood what it meant to regard others as more important than himself; and more than that, he practiced it. He generously gave himself away in caring for the needs of others. That's why Paul felt comfortable sending Timothy to Philippi. "You get Timothy—you get me" was Paul's opinion. And that made his heart as well as his chains a little lighter.

### A "Brother" Named Epaphroditus

The second close friend Paul mentions in his letter is Epaphroditus.

> But I thought it necessary to send to you Epaphroditus, my brother and fellow worker and fellow soldier, who is also your messenger and minister to my need; because he was longing for you all and was distressed because you had heard that he was sick. For indeed he was sick to the point of death, but God had mercy on him, and not on him only but also on me, lest I should have sorrow upon sorrow. Therefore I have sent him all the more eagerly in order that when you see him again you may rejoice and I may be less concerned about you. Therefore receive him in the Lord with all joy, and hold men like him in high regard; because he came close to death for the work of Christ, risking his life to complete what was deficient in your service to me. (vv. 25–30)

The problem with reading someone else's mail, especially when it was written centuries ago, is that we don't always know the circumstances surrounding a story. In this case, who was Epaphroditus? How did he and Paul meet? Questions like these need answering before we can fully appreciate what Paul says about this special friend. So let's back up, with commentator William Barclay's help, and find out the dramatic story behind Paul's glowing words.

> When the Philippians heard that Paul was in prison, their warm hearts were moved to action. They sent a gift to him by the hand of Epaphroditus. What they could not personally do, because distance prevented them, they delegated to Epaphroditus to do for them. Not only did they intend him to be the

bearer of their gift; they also intended him to stay in Rome and be Paul's personal servant and attendant. Clearly Epaphroditus was a brave man, for any one who proposed to offer himself as the personal attendant of a man awaiting trial on a capital charge was laying himself open to the very considerable risk of becoming involved in the same charge. In truth, Epaphroditus risked his life to serve Paul.

In Rome Epaphroditus fell ill, perhaps with the notorious Roman fever which sometimes swept the city like a scourge, and was near to death. He knew that news of his illness had filtered back to Philippi, and he was worried because he knew that his friends there would be worried about him. God in his mercy spared the life of Epaphroditus and so spared Paul yet more sorrow. But Paul knew that it was time that Epaphroditus went back home, and in all probability he was the bearer of this letter.

But there was a problem. The Philippian Church had sent Epaphroditus to stay with Paul, and if he came back home, there would not be lacking those who said that he was a quitter. Here Paul gives him a tremendous testimonial, which will silence any possible criticism of his return.[2]

Now, perhaps, we can understand why Paul uses so many word pictures—"brother," "fellow worker," "fellow soldier," "messenger," "minister to my need" (v. 25)—to describe this dear friend. Epaphroditus was one in common sympathy, common work, and common danger with the great Apostle.[3]

Having such a friend near must surely have given Paul great joy. So why did he send him back? First of all, to ease the minds of the believers back home in Philippi (vv. 25–27). And second, to cause them to rejoice, which would lessen Paul's concern over them (v. 28). At the same time, Paul gave clear instructions on what he felt their response to Epaphroditus should be. They were to extend

2. William Barclay, *The Letters to the Philippians, Colossians, and Thessalonians*, rev. ed., The Daily Study Bible Series (Philadelphia, Pa.: Westminster Press, 1975), pp. 48–49.

3. See Bishop Lightfoot, as quoted by Barclay in *Philippians, Colossians, and Thessalonians*, p. 49.

a joyful welcome and hold him in high regard (v. 29). Why? Because he had risked his life in fulfilling his mission (v. 30).

In Greek, the term Paul used for *risking* is *parabouleuomai*, which means "to hazard one's life, to gamble." Epaphroditus did exactly that. He gambled with his life in associating with Paul. And his service and sacrifice became an example that was copied by others.

> In the early church there were societies of men and women who called themselves *the parabolani*, that is, *the riskers or gamblers*. They ministered to the sick and imprisoned, and they saw to it that, if at all possible, martyrs and sometimes even enemies would receive an honorable burial. Thus in the city of Carthage during the great pestilence of A.D. 252 Cyprian, the bishop, showed remarkable courage. In self-sacrificing fidelity to his flock, and love even for his enemies, he took upon himself the care of the sick, and bade his congregation nurse them and bury the dead. What a contrast with the practice of the heathen who were throwing the corpses out of the plague-stricken city and were running away in terror![4]

Epaphroditus was the forerunner of the *parabolani*. Not even the threat of death could hold him back. Such love and reckless devotion certainly won Paul's respect, and he wanted the church in Philippi to share this same respect for their beloved brother.

## Three People Who Deserve a Response

By way of application, let's consider three categories of special people and how we are to respond to them.

First, *when God sends a Timothy into our lives, He expects us to relate to him.* Such kindred spirits can be a source of deep joy in our lives if we will but cultivate them.

Second, *when God sends an Epaphroditus to minister to us, He expects us to respect him.* The next time people come to your assistance with nothing to gain but perhaps much to lose, don't try to repay them—respect them. That's the best response you could give.

The third special person for us to consider is One whose friendship is available to everyone at any time—Jesus. *Since God sent*

---

4. William Hendriksen, *New Testament Commentary: Exposition of Philippians* (Grand Rapids, Mich.: Baker Book House, 1962), pp. 144–45.

*Christ to take away our sins and bring us to heaven, He expects us to receive Him.* It's amazing how many of us eagerly relate to a Timothy and respect an Epaphroditus yet refuse to receive Jesus. These other relationships are wonderful, but they cannot offer the forgiveness and joy that only Jesus can give. All of us need a Savior. When God introduces you to Him, choose the one response that's appropriate—receive.

> But as many as received Him, to them He gave the right to become children of God, even to those who believe in His name. (John 1:12)

## 🍇 Living Insights

In his book *Quality Friendship,* Gary Inrig writes:

> Out of the furnaces of war come many true stories of sacrificial friendship. One such story tells of two friends in World War I, who were inseparable. They had enlisted together, trained together, were shipped overseas together, and fought side-by-side in the trenches. During an attack, one of the men was critically wounded in a field filled with barbed wire obstacles, and he was unable to crawl back to his foxhole. The entire area was under a withering enemy crossfire, and it was suicidal to try to reach him. Yet his friend decided to try. Before he could get out of his own trench, his sergeant yanked him back inside and ordered him not to go. "It's too late. You can't do him any good, and you'll only get yourself killed."
>
> A few minutes later, the officer turned his back, and instantly the man was gone after his friend. A few minutes later, he staggered back, mortally wounded, with his friend, now dead, in his arms. The sergeant was both angry and deeply moved. "What a waste," he blurted out. "He's dead and you're dying. It just wasn't worth it."
>
> With almost his last breath, the dying man replied, "Oh, yes, it was, Sarge. When I got to him, the only thing he said was, 'I knew you'd come, Jim!'"
>
> One of the marks of a true friend is that he is there when there is every reason for him not to be,

when to be there is sacrificially costly. As Proverbs 17:17 puts it, "A friend loves at all times, and a brother is born for adversity."[5]

Epaphroditus was there for Paul when it was costly. All true friends are. Is that same mark of commitment and loyalty evident in the way you relate to your close friends? For help in finding out, spend some time thinking through the following questions.

1. What are the limits of my friendship? Do I use people, or do I lay down my life for them? How much do I know of sacrificial love?
2. What is my impact on others? Am I a change agent for godliness in my friend's life? Is he more of a disciple because of me? Am I giving away myself in such a way that God-given needs are being met in his life?
3. Do I take the risk of openness, or is there a carefully constructed wall around my life that no one can penetrate? Have I ever expressed verbally my love and appreciation for my friend and displayed that love by opening up my life to him?
4. Am I an initiator of love, or am I waiting for others to earn my approval or to reach out to me? . . .
5. How am I helping my friend realize his potential in any or every area of life? Is he fruitful because of me?[6]

### 🍇 *Living Insights*             STUDY TWO

In everyone's life, there are basically three levels of relationships: acquaintance, casual, and intimate.

5. Gary Inrig, *Quality Friendship* (Chicago, Ill.: Moody Press, 1981), pp. 73–74.
6. Inrig, *Quality Friendship*, p. 23.

Pause and study this simple diagram for a moment. Think about the kinds of activities, amount of time spent, level of communication, degree of openness, emotional involvement, depth of satisfaction, and number of people at each of these levels.

Once you feel you have a thorough understanding of these three kinds of friendships, put yourself in the middle of that diagram and ask, What names belong on each level in my life?

Acquaintance _____

_____

_____

Casual _____

_____

Intimate _____

If Paul were to fill this out, Timothy would certainly be one of the special friends listed on the intimate level. Kindred spirits like that don't come along very often. They seem to become even rarer the older and busier we become. Alan Loy McGinnis writes:

> Some people immerse themselves in such a whirl of parties and social affairs that there is no opportunity to establish a close relationship. The fact of the matter is that one cannot have a profound connection with more than a few people. Time prohibits it. . . . If your social calendar is too full to provide for such intimate bonding, it should be pared. "True happiness," said Ben Jonson, "consists not in the multitude of friends, but in the worth and choice."[7]

Are you neglecting to cultivate or maintain intimate friendships because you're too busy? Is having a best friend a priority?

When this year is over, what gift will your current schedule present you with? The popularity to receive hundreds of Christmas cards from acquaintances only? Or the deeper satisfaction and joy of a few close friendships as well?

7. Alan Loy McGinnis, *The Friendship Factor* (Minneapolis, Minn.: Augsburg Publishing House, 1979), p. 24.

## Chapter 8

# HAPPY HOPES FOR HIGH ACHIEVERS

*Philippians 3:1–11*

In a society obsessed with high achievers, children quickly learn that to be recognized, praised, and rewarded they have to perform well. They cut their teeth on the hard fact that this world assigns value to people based on their success. Self-worth is something that has to be earned. And you do that by achieving more than many so that you can be recognized as being better than most.

## The Great Temptation among High Achievers

To one degree or another, we've all been raised on this philosophy of achievement. It's in our blood to believe that accomplishments will bring us recognition and lasting joy in the here and now—and maybe even in the hereafter. Therein lies the great temptation that hounds high achievers.

### What Is It?

This temptation is the belief that earthly achievements can merit the heavenly reward of salvation. We think that if we work hard enough, if our good outweighs our bad, God will surely award us the keys to His kingdom.

The obvious problem with this kind of thinking, besides the fact that it is not biblical, is that no one can see this supposed heavenly scale that holds our life in its balance. At best, we can only guess whether or not it is tipped in our favor. So life is reduced to a constant seesaw struggle for salvation motivated by a fear that enough is never enough. We must always work harder and do more.

### Why Does It Happen?

At the heart of our efforts to earn God's approval is *pride*. We believe that if we can earn the world's top honors, then we can certainly meet God's standard of righteousness. Rather than glorifying God, this is just another way of glorifying ourselves. And the harder we try, the more joyless and judgmental we become.

Perhaps no one knew this better than the apostle Paul, who was once a proud Pharisee—the ultimate high achiever. Before his conversion, he was driven to gain a righteousness of his own through the works of the Law. But then Saul of Tarsus met the Lord Jesus. And, as we shall see in his letter today, that changed everything.

## The Honest Testimony of a High-Achieving Pharisee

Paul begins this section of his Philippian letter with a reaffirmation of his theme.

> Finally, my brethren, rejoice in the Lord. To write the same things again is no trouble to me, and it is a safeguard for you. (Phil. 3:1)

Why did Paul feel that his joyful reminder was a "safeguard"? Because not only were the pressures of life enough to steal the Philippians' joy, there were also legalists afoot who dogged Paul's message of grace everywhere he preached it. Even as he wrote, the Apostle knew that these joy stealers called Judaizers were there in Philippi, hounding the believers to live under the Law instead of rejoicing in the grace they received in Christ. "To be saved and live the Christian life, you have to become like Jews," they said. "Everyone must learn to eat a certain diet and observe certain rituals. You Greek men must be circumcised and you women must learn how to conduct yourself according to our strict traditions."

### A Warning to His Close Friends

The threat posed by the Judaizers to the Philippians' spiritual growth and joy was serious. So serious that the Apostle denounces them to his readers with not one or two, but three disparaging descriptions.

> Beware of the dogs, beware of the evil workers, beware of the false circumcision. (v. 2)

When Paul compares the legalists to dogs, he's not thinking of the pampered pets we have these days. Dogs in the first century were dirty, disease-carrying scavengers that ran in wild packs. They were uncontrolled and potentially dangerous to anyone who got in their way. So Paul warns them through this image to guard against those snarling legalists that scavenge for converts to devour with their fatal false doctrines.

Paul also calls the Judaizers "evil workers" because they sowed the corrupt gospel that people are saved by faith plus works of the Law. The good news of Jesus Christ, however, is that works are the result of—not the means to—receiving salvation. Paul would not have his beloved laboring under the shame and obligation that come from never knowing how much is enough to satisfy God. He wants them free to rejoice in what God has done for them—a radically different perspective.

Then, using a play on words, the Apostle labels the legalists as the "false circumcision"; people who "mutilated the gospel by insisting on the need to mutilate the flesh in order to be rightly related to God."[1]

With firm assurance then, Paul concludes his warning with a contrast.

> For we are the true circumcision, who worship in
> the Spirit of God and glory in Christ Jesus and put
> no confidence in the flesh. (v. 3)

Paul sees three basic differences between true believers and high-achievement Judaizers. First, believers "worship in the Spirit of God"—meaning their focus is kept on God's divine work, not human achievement. Second, unlike the Judaizers who boast in their works, Christians glory in the person and work of Jesus Christ. And third, Christ's followers "put no confidence in the flesh." Salvation through human works? Not a chance. Pride in personal piety? Absolutely not. Their only confidence is in Jesus.

### A Revealing of His Proud Record

When it came to talking about confidence in the flesh, no one was better qualified to speak than this ex-Pharisee, whose religious trophy case contained more achievements than any of his contemporaries.

> If anyone else has a mind to put confidence in the
> flesh, I far more: circumcised the eighth day, of the
> nation of Israel, of the tribe of Benjamin, a Hebrew
> of Hebrews; as to the Law, a Pharisee; as to zeal, a
> persecutor of the church; as to the righteousness
> which is in the Law, found blameless. (vv. 4b–6)

---

1. Robert P. Lightner, "Philippians," in *The Bible Knowledge Commentary*, New Testament ed., ed. John F. Walvoord and Roy B. Zuck (Wheaton, Ill.: SP Publications, Victor Books, 1983), p. 659.

This centuries-old resume may not sound all that impressive today, but it was highly significant to a first-century Jew. Let's enter into the meaning of Paul's words with the help of commentator William Barclay.

> If ever there was a Jew who was steeped in Juda-
> ism, that Jew was Paul. Let us . . . look again at the
> claims he had to be the Jew *par excellence*. . . . He
> was circumcised on the eighth day; that is to say, he
> bore in the body the badge and the mark that he
> was one of the chosen people, marked out by God
> as His own. He was of the race of Israel; that is to
> say, he was a member of the nation who stood in a
> covenant relationship with God, a relationship in
> which no other people stood. He was of the tribe of
> Benjamin. . . . What is the point of this claim? The
> tribe of Benjamin had a unique place in the history
> of Israel. It was from Benjamin that the first king
> of Israel had come, for Saul was a Benjamite. . . .
> Benjamin was the only one of the patriarchs who
> had actually been born in the land of promise. When
> Israel went into battle, it was the tribe of Benjamin
> which held the post of honor. The battle-cry of Israel
> was: "After thee, O Benjamin." . . .
> In lineage Paul was not only an Israelite; he was
> of the aristocracy of Israel. He was a Hebrew of the
> Hebrews; that is to say, Paul was not one of these
> Jews of the Dispersion who, in a foreign land, had
> forgotten their own tongue; he was a Jew who still
> remembered and knew the language of his fathers.
> He was a Pharisee; that is to say, he was not only
> a devout Jew; he was more—he was one of "The
> Separated Ones" who had foresworn all normal ac-
> tivities in order to dedicate life to the keeping of
> the Law, and he had kept it with such meticulous
> care that in the keeping of it he was blameless.[2]

Did you notice how Paul categorized his achievements? "As to the Law . . . as to zeal . . . as to righteousness." Add them all up,

---

2. William Barclay, *The Mind of St. Paul* (New York, N.Y.: Harper and Row, Publishers, 1958), pp. 17–19.

and the scales of human achievement would register "blameless." According to the Law, Saul of Tarsus was the model Pharisee, a paragon of human perfection.

### A Change in His Entire Life

But when that paragon took off for Damascus on another of his zealous trips to persecute Christians, his whole life was suddenly changed. A blazing light from heaven blinded him in an instant, and he heard a voice saying, "Saul, Saul, why are you persecuting Me?" (see Acts 9:1–4). Bewildered and afraid, Saul asked,

> "Who art Thou, Lord?" And He said, "I am Jesus whom you are persecuting." (v. 5)

It was a humbling moment for that proud Pharisee. A crossroad where he took his first baby steps toward realizing that all his self-righteous achievements were nothing more than dirty rags to God (Isa. 64:6).

Since that unexpected epiphany, Paul has seen his personal achievements from a completely different perspective.

> But whatever things were gain to me, those things I have counted as loss for the sake of Christ. More than that I count all things to be loss in view of the surpassing value of knowing Christ Jesus my Lord, for whom I have suffered the loss of all things, and count them but rubbish in order that I may gain Christ, and may be found in Him, not having a righteousness of my own derived from the Law, but that which is through faith in Christ, the righteousness which comes from God on the basis of faith. (Phil. 3:7–9)

All the awards, applause, victories, and credits that were once the foundation of his righteousness and pride are gone, changed, removed. In fact, Paul calls them "rubbish." The Greek term for this is used only here in all the New Testament. In its root form, it could mean either "excrement," "dung," or "trash, the kind thrown to the dogs."[3] In place of the proud, self-achieving Pharisee now lived a humble believer who admitted his neediness and spiritual

---

3. See William Hendriksen, *New Testament Commentary: Exposition of Philippians* (Grand Rapids, Mich.: Baker Book House, 1962), p. 164.

bankruptcy. And God in His grace credited his faith with the perfect righteousness of His Son.

### A Statement of His Consuming Passion

Once the Apostle began trusting in God's righteous Son for salvation instead of trusting in good works, the passion in his life completely changed. No longer did he hunger for earthly applause; instead, his goal was that he might

> know Him, and the power of His resurrection and the fellowship of His sufferings, being conformed to His death; in order that I may attain to the resurrection from the dead. (vv. 10–11)

These are the hopes of a born-again high achiever: to know Christ more intimately, to draw upon His resurrection power more increasingly, to enter into His suffering more personally, and to be conformed to His image more completely.

## The Plain Truth to All Who Respond

Simply stated, the two truths reflected in the life of the apostle Paul before and after his Damascus road conversion are:

• First, *trusting in your own achievements brings you glory now, but leaves you spiritually bankrupt forever.*

• And second, *trusting in Christ's accomplishment gives Him the glory now, and results in your eternal righteousness forever.*

Won't you put down that report card you've been carrying around and begin basking in the light of God's merciful righteousness today?

🍇 *Living Insights* STUDY ONE

From the time Paul put his trust in Jesus for salvation instead of in his own accomplishments, his new consuming passion was, in part, to be conformed to Christ's death (Phil. 3:10). A strange-sounding goal for such a hard-charging high achiever. What does it mean? The Apostle himself explains in his letter to the Romans.

> What shall we say then? Are we to continue in sin that grace might increase? May it never be! How shall we who died to sin still live in it? Or do you

not know that all of us who have been baptized into Christ Jesus have been baptized into His death? Therefore we have been buried with Him through baptism into death, in order that as Christ was raised from the dead through the glory of the Father, so we too might walk in newness of life. For if we have become united with Him in the likeness of His death, certainly we shall be also in the likeness of His resurrection, knowing this, that our old self was crucified with Him, that our body of sin might be done away with, that we should no longer be slaves to sin. (6:1–11)

For Paul, being conformed to Jesus' death meant becoming dead to sin and self-centeredness. In this way, Paul could be a blessing to others, just as Christ was in His death. Easily said, but not easily done. Especially for people whose attitude toward sin is more self-centered than Christ-centered. In his book *The Pursuit of Holiness*, Jerry Bridges elaborates on this problem, which is particularly common among high achievers.

> We are more concerned about our own "victory" over sin than we are about the fact that our sins grieve the heart of God. We cannot tolerate failure in our struggle with sin chiefly because we are success-oriented, not because we know it is offensive to God. . . .
>
> God wants us to walk in *obedience*—not victory. Obedience is oriented toward God; victory is oriented toward self. This may seem to be merely splitting hairs over semantics, but there is a subtle, self-centered attitude at the root of many of our difficulties with sin. . . .
>
> This is not to say God doesn't want us to experience victory, but rather to emphasize that victory is a by-product of obedience. As we concentrate on living an obedient, holy life, we will certainly experience the joy of victory over sin.[4]

Are you feeling defeated in your efforts to follow Paul's credo and die to sin? Could it be that your focus is on victory rather than

4. Jerry Bridges, *The Pursuit of Holiness* (Colorado Springs, Colo.: NavPress, 1978), pp. 20–21.

on obedience? Is it possible that the pride of high achievement has turned your struggle against sin into a self-centered pursuit rather than a God-centered passion?

If so, start practicing a new, biblical attitude toward sin by focusing on obedience rather than victory. Let your passion be for knowing Christ, not for earning an impressive collection of spiritual achievements.

## Living Insights

Ask a lot of people in church as well as out if they think they'll go to heaven when they die, and you'll probably hear something like,

"Well, I've tried very hard to be a good person."

What do people mean when they say that? Most people would explain it this way:

"All my life I've tried to love others like I would want them to love me. I'm fair, treat others with respect, volunteer to help the needy, and give what I can to the church and other good organizations that help people. And I've never done anything wrong, that is, nothing really bad deserving of God's judgment, like killing someone. So yeah, I think I'll go to heaven. I hope."

Imagine for a moment that this is a close personal friend speaking to you. How would you respond? What is it that you've learned from our lesson that could be applied here? Before answering, spend some time studying the following Scriptures or any others you might think helpful, then write down your response in the space provided.

Scriptures: Isaiah 64:6; James 2:10; Romans 3,5; Ephesians 2:4–9; John 14:6

Additional passages: _____

### Response

_____

_____

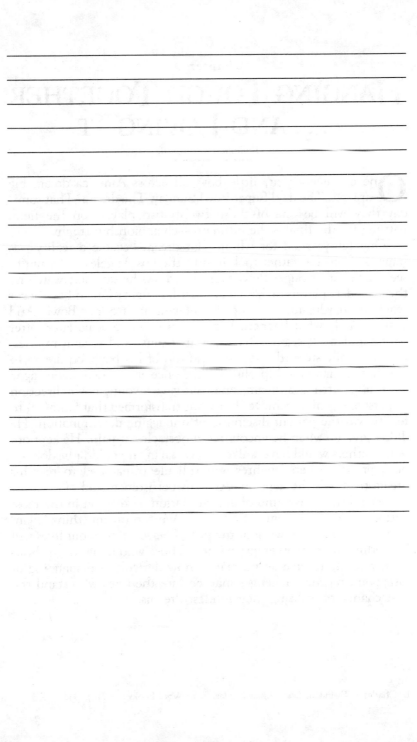

## Chapter 9

# HANGING TOUGH TOGETHER ...AND LOVING IT

### Philippians 3:12–16

One day every year, little boys all across America dream big dreams. The day? Super Bowl Sunday. The dream? That some-day they will be one of those twenty-two players on the field, battling for the final—the ultimate—championship trophy.

One ten-year-old for whom that dream became a reality was James Lofton. His father took him to the Los Angeles Coliseum to see the very first Super Bowl ever played. As he sat there watching the legendary players on Vince Lombardi's mighty Green Bay Packer team, he daydreamed of one day playing in a Super Bowl. And that's exactly what happened. Some twenty-five years later, after strong and weak seasons, changes in teams, and several injuries, Lofton finally stepped onto the gridiron of his boyhood dream to play in the championship game he had once envisioned so long ago.[1]

It all started as a dream, one that gave a young boy a direction to pursue, a goal to achieve. But what transformed that fantasy into reality was the patient discipline of unflagging determination. He didn't give up when he encountered obstacles or pain. He kept on. When others would have walked away, saying it couldn't be done— he kept on. When laughter and ridicule threatened to tear his dream to shreds, he kept on. And his persistence paid off.

We all need that kind of determination to keep on in the most daring and difficult game of all—life. We can dream, think, plan, hope, even pray; but without the grit of perseverance, our lives will be nothing more than empty wishes. Those who hang tough, how-ever, refusing to give up no matter how difficult or demanding or disappointing the challenges may be, are the ones who stand the best chance of realizing their fondest dreams.

---

1. Charles R. Swindoll, *Laugh Again* (Dallas, Tex.: Word Books, 1992), p. 143.

## A Brief Stop at Today's Shelves

Interestingly, the popular message communicated by many of today's management and motivational books isn't about hard work and hanging tough over the long haul. Society's feelings toward long-term diligence have changed. Nowadays, what you see as you browse the bookstores are eye-catching, cleverly worded titles that promise microwavable success—the kind where you follow a few simple instructions and are instantly rewarded. Life made quick and easy. In reality, however, about the only thing quick or easy is the buck authors make selling such pied piper promises.

Ask the athlete striving to win the gold or the young woman earning a Ph.D. or the musician perfecting his skill, and each will tell you there is no secret for quick success. The plain truth is that whether we're attempting to master our bodies, a subject, or an instrument, the requirement is the same: a relentless pursuit of the right objectives.

That same basic requirement is on Paul's mind as he writes about living the Christian life in the third chapter of his letter to the Philippians. There are no slick, book jacket promises in the Apostle's words, no quick-and-easy secrets for becoming like Christ. Only the determined advice to keep on . . . even when we encounter obstacles, even when there is pain, doubt, and ridicule. And by God's grace, that persistence will pay off with the kind of prize Paul himself pursued—Christlikeness.

## A Lingering Look at Paul's Prescription

As we saw in our last lesson, once Paul encountered Christ on the road to Damascus, his whole life was transformed. He quit trusting in his religious heritage, schooling, achievements, and zeal for personal righteousness and received the righteousness that comes through faith in Christ.

But where does someone like Paul go from there? Had he "arrived" spiritually? Was that all there was to the Christian life? Hardly. For the Apostle, the pursuit of his newfound dream of Christlikeness had only just begun. To make that dream a reality, he, too, began a relentless pursuit of right objectives. In his own words, he began to "press on."

> Not that I have already obtained it, or have already
> become perfect, but I press on in order that I may
> lay hold of that for which also I was laid hold of by

Christ Jesus. Brethren, I do not regard myself as having laid hold of it yet; but one thing I do: forgetting what lies behind and reaching forward to what lies ahead, I press on toward the goal for the prize of the upward call of God in Christ Jesus. Let us therefore, as many as are perfect, have this attitude; and if in anything you have a different attitude, God will reveal that also to you; however, let us keep living by that same standard to which we have attained. (Phil. 3:12–16)

To find out more about what it means to press on toward the prize of becoming like Christ, let's look at five things Paul felt were important.

### 1. The Plan Is Progress . . . Not Perfection

Not that I have already obtained it, or have already become perfect. . . . I do not regard myself as having laid hold of it yet. (vv. 12a, 13a)

With not one but two admissions about his own imperfections, the Apostle makes clear that it's progress that works as a plan for living, not perfection.

Making progress, pressing on, is not always easy, however. It can be painful and disappointing at times because of the imperfection we live with as humans. Not only are we imperfect, but so is everyone around us. We cannot escape our own fallible humanity in this fallen world. Some of us get so intense in our pursuit of godliness, though, that we get frustrated and down on ourselves when we fail. That's when we most need to remember that the plan is progress, not perfection. Learn to press on in spite of the lack of perfection. If you can see changes in your life as compared to where you were a year ago, take heart—you are on the right road!

### 2. The Past Is Over . . . Forget It!

Forgetting what lies behind . . . (v. 13b)

Another important piece of advice Paul gives for hanging tough over the long haul is to forget what lies behind. To emphasize his point, he uses a Greek word for *forgetting* that means "absolute and complete" forgetting. In the ancient world, this term was used of a runner who passed another in a race. Once in front, the lead runner didn't look back. He forgot what lay behind him and kept his focus solely on the tape in front of him.

If we are to press on toward the eternal tape in front of us, we must refuse to focus on yesterday. No looking back over our shoulders at either accomplishments or failures gone by. To glory in past achievements only makes us proud and perhaps indifferent to what lies ahead. And to torture ourselves with former mistakes only arouses guilt and shame, weakening our courage for upcoming challenges. Paul says to forget the past. Focus on the tape, the goal, Jesus!

### 3. The Future Holds Out Hope . . . Reach for It!

Reaching forward to what lies ahead . . . (v. 13c)

Paul may well have had in mind the Olympic chariot races in ancient Greece when he wrote this counsel. Standing on a small platform and leaning forward, the charioteer strained his muscles both to keep his balance and to control his horses. In doing so, he stretched himself as he drove hard to win. In the same way, we, too, are to stretch ourselves, to lean forward with the same intensity toward "the prize of the upward call of God in Christ Jesus" (v. 14).

Does that describe you? Are you making some kind of deliberate progress with your life? Do you passionately pursue godliness? Remember, the Christian life was never meant to be a peaceful alliance or passive coexistence with enemy forces. It's to be a passionate quest, ever stretching and reaching for the prize.

### 4. The Secret Is a Determined Attitude . . . Maintain It!

Let us therefore, as many as are perfect, have this attitude. (v. 15a)

And yet which of us is qualified to maintain a determined attitude if we have to be "perfect"? Commentator Stuart Briscoe helps untangle the confusion by explaining that the word *perfect* used here doesn't mean without sin; it simply means "mature" or "complete." In other words, "I am complete in the sense that I have grown as far as I can at the present, and I am ready for the next lesson."[2] That best defines a determined attitude.

Notice also one very important point communicated in the latter half of this verse: "If in anything you have a different attitude, God will reveal that also to you" (v. 15b). Graciously, Paul gives others the liberty to grow at their own pace. Paul never holds out

---

2. Stuart Briscoe, *Bound for Joy* (Ventura, Calif.: Regal Books, 1975), p. 129.

hoops for everyone to jump through mechanically; life is so much more varied and rich than that. Instead, he relaxes in God's ability to shape a person the way He wants.

### 5. The Need Is Keeping a High Standard . . . Together

> Let us keep living by that same standard to which we have attained. (v. 16)

Notice how the Apostle shifts the focus from himself, "I press on" (vv. 12, 14), to all believers, "let us" press on (vv. 15–16). Living the Christian life is a mutual effort, not a solo mission. There is great comfort and strength to be gained if we will lock arms with those who are striving to keep the same high standard.

## A Random Sampling of Biblical Examples

Just a cursory glance at the landscape of biblical history reveals deep valleys of those who did not press on . . . and peaks of individuals who did.

On the negative side, think of Lot, who had so much going for him but lost sight of the goal. Think of Samson, who judged Israel for twenty years but preferred the embrace of a harlot and finished blind and bound. Think of Saul, the king whom God elected but later rejected because of his disobedience. And many others, like Jonah, the reluctant prophet, and Ananias and Sapphira, who lied to God because of their greed.

On the encouraging side, let your eyes focus on Joseph, who pressed on despite unfair circumstances and kept his hope firmly fixed on the Lord. Remember Daniel, who maintained a determined attitude in a foreign land. Consider John Mark, who stumbled momentarily as a missionary, but later distinguished himself as Paul's helper. Then, too, don't forget about Moses, whom God used in spite of his early failure. What better example of the principle that pressing on means progress, not perfection.

## A Workable Plan for Everyday Living

If we were to take these five principles from Philippians and meld them together into a workable plan—something to help us hang tough as we relentlessly pursue Christ—it would read like this:

Progress is maintained by:

*Forgetting yesterday's glory and grind*
*and by*

74

*Focusing on tomorrow's challenging opportunities*
*while we*
*Keep the right attitude and remember*
*we are in it together.* [3]

There's no better way to hang tough . . . and love it!

## 🍇 *Living Insights* STUDY ONE

Nothing can be accomplished without the patient discipline of unflagging determination. As William Barclay wrote, "Many an athlete and many a man has been ruined because he abandoned discipline and let himself grow slack."[4] One such man was Samuel Taylor Coleridge.

> Never did so great a mind produce so little. He left Cambridge University to join the army; he left the army because, in spite of all his erudition, he could not rub down a horse; he returned to Oxford and left without a degree. He began a paper called *The Watchman* which lived for ten numbers and then died. It has been said of him: "He lost himself in visions of work to be done, that always remained to be done. Coleridge had every poetic gift but one— the gift of sustained and concentrated effort." In his head and in his mind he had all kinds of books, as he said, himself, "completed save for transcription." "I am on the eve," he says, "of sending to the press two octavo volumes." But the books were never composed outside Coleridge's mind, because he would not face the discipline of sitting down to write them out.[5]

Always beginning, but never finishing. Coleridge lacked that one essential ingredient that could have turned his dreams into reality and kept them there—determination.

---

3. Swindoll, *Laugh Again*, p. 154.

4. William Barclay, *The Gospel of Matthew*, vol. 1, rev. ed., The Daily Study Bible Series (Philadelphia, Pa.: Westminster Press, 1975), p. 280.

5. Barclay, *The Gospel of Matthew*, p. 280.

Many of us are lacking that same key ingredient in our pursuit of Christ. Like Coleridge, we are always "on the eve" of getting serious, but then never do because we lack a sustained and concentrated effort.

Is there something holding you back? Is it failure? Are you afraid to pursue Christ because you know before you even begin that you're going to make mistakes? Or perhaps you are preoccupied with past mistakes, thinking that you've made so many already—what's the use of trying again? That's the perfectionist in you talking. But remember, as Paul said, the plan is progress, not perfection. God's forgiveness and love are there to help you get up and continue your determined pursuit of Him.

Perhaps you're having trouble hanging tough simply because you've never fully committed yourself to becoming like Christ. If you feel that you're lacking the patient discipline of unflagging determination, go back over the five principles in the lesson and see if you can discover what might be blocking you from making that commitment.

Don't skip ahead and skip out here. Remember: "No one ever reached any eminence, and no one having reached it ever maintained it, without discipline."[6]

_____

_____

_____

 *Living Insights* STUDY TWO

Progress is maintained by:

*Forgetting yesterday's glory and grind*
*and by*
*Focusing on tomorrow's challenging opportunities*
*while we*
*Keep the right attitude and remember*
*we are in it together.*

6. Barclay, *The Gospel of Matthew*, p. 280.

Many Christians are going to drift from their pursuit of Christ today—not because they couldn't forget yesterday's glory and grind, not because they couldn't focus on tomorrow's challenging opportunities, not because they didn't have the right attitude—but because, simply, they are in it *alone*.

The apostle Paul was an incredible individual, but do you think he could have endured all the adversities he faced and still relentlessly pursued Christ if he had been alone the whole way? It's doubtful. He was human just like the rest of us; and he needed Timothys and Epaphrodituses, just like we do, to run the race and not drop out before it was over.

It takes more than just being theologically correct and spiritually enthusiastic to hang tough over the long haul; it takes the support of close companions.

Stop for a moment. Look around. Who's there to help when you get winded and weary?

_____

_____

Who are you looking out for?

_____

_____

## Chapter 10

# IT'S A MAD, BAD, SAD WORLD, BUT . . .

### Philippians 3:17–4:1

The role of the Christian is unusual. Some would even say it's just plain weird! And you know, from a strictly human perspective, they're right. As A. W. Tozer pointed out:

> A real Christian is an odd number anyway. He feels supreme love for One whom he has never seen, talks familiarly every day to Someone he cannot see, expects to go to heaven on the virtue of Another, empties himself in order to be full, admits he is wrong so he can be declared right, goes down in order to get up, is strongest when he is weakest, richest when he is poorest, and happiest when he feels worst. He dies so he can live, forsakes in order to have, gives away so he can keep, sees the invisible, hears the inaudible, and knows that which passeth knowledge.[1]

Convincing, isn't he? Christians really are an odd number. Why? Because of a unique and unusual relationship with the living God. Through faith in Christ we have been born into God's eternal family. Now our true home and citizenship is in heaven. Yet we still must live on earth . . . and that poses a problem: how to be in the world, but not of it.

Even though the earth may not be our home, it is our current residence. And living here, we face a powerful pressure to abandon our heavenly Father and adopt the prodigal lifestyle of a lost and rebellious world. Which raises the question, Why does God leave us in such a hostile environment? Why doesn't He move His own into heaven just as soon as they're converted?

---

1. A. W. Tozer, *The Root of the Righteous* (Harrisburg, Pa.: Christian Publications, 1955), p. 156.

## Our Lord's Strange Strategy

Leaving heaven-bound people in a hell-bound world is not a simple oversight on the Lord's part. He has a reason, a plan; yes, you might even say a strange strategy for His unusual followers. One that His Son revealed to His disciples during their last supper together. Distilled, Jesus' counsel can be summed up in three definitive statements.

First, *we can have inner peace in the midst of outer pressure and pain.* Listen carefully as Jesus describes the pain and the peace.

> "These things I have spoken to you, that you may be kept from stumbling. They will make you outcasts from the synagogue, but an hour is coming for everyone who kills you to think that he is offering service to God." (John 16:1–2)

> "But when He, the Spirit of truth, comes, He will guide you into all the truth; for He will not speak on His own initiative, but whatever He hears, He will speak; and He will disclose to you what is to come." (v. 13)

> "These things I have spoken to you, that in Me you may have peace. In the world you have tribulation, but take courage; I have overcome the world." (v. 33)

Does Christ promise an easygoing, laid-back existence? We only wish He did! Instead He just guarantees suffering and pain for His disciples. Christians can be treated unfairly. We can be abused and neglected. We can lose all our savings in a scam or be robbed or raped. Yet even in the worst of life's circumstances, a deep, inner peace is available to those who trust in Christ. Not a peace that erases the pain; rather, a peace that supernaturally enables Christians to endure in it. A peace that offers assurance, hope, even joy amidst adversity.

Second, *we are insulated by divine power, yet we are not to live an isolated existence.* Again let's listen to Jesus, this time as He prays for His disciples.

> "And I am no more in the world; and yet they themselves are in the world, and I come to Thee. Holy Father, keep them in Thy name, the name which Thou hast given Me, that they may be one, even as

We are. While I was with them, I was keeping them in Thy name which Thou hast given Me; and I guarded them, and not one of them perished but the son of perdition, that the Scripture might be fulfilled. But now I come to Thee; and these things I speak in the world, that they may have My joy made full in themselves. I have given them Thy word; and the world has hated them, because they are not of the world, even as I am not of the world. I do not ask Thee to take them out of the world, but to keep them from the evil one." (17:11–15)

Christ's prayer is not that we be kept from evil, but from the Evil One. This sinful world isn't something we are to avoid by cloistering ourselves behind sanctimonious walls of self-righteousness. That's taking ourselves out of the world. Rather, Jesus wants us in the world so that His light will shine in the darkness where Satan rules over the lost. So don't withdraw; reach out—with Christ's power and His protection.

And third, *we may be unique, but we must be unified.* This, too, comes from Jesus' prayer in the Upper Room.

"They are not of the world, even as I am not of the world. Sanctify them in the truth; Thy word is truth. . . . That they may all be one; even as Thou, Father, art in Me, and I in Thee, that they also may be in Us; that the world may believe that Thou didst send Me. . . . I in them, and Thou in Me, that they may be perfected in unity, that the world may know that Thou didst send Me, and didst love them, even as Thou didst love Me." (vv. 16–17, 21, 23)

God is pleased to use each of us individually to draw others to Himself, but that is only part of His strategy. He also wants to use our unity in Christ, our sense of community, as a powerful witness to awaken the lost to their neediness, pointing them to the Father who loved them through the sacrifice of His Son.

## The Christian's Marching Orders

Ours truly is a mad, bad, sad world—but—it is not impossible to reach. The apostle Paul knew that. Time and again he saw God's strategy work effectively in bringing the lost to Christ. He saw it at work in the church at Philippi, for example. The people there knew pain and yet also knew peace. They lived insulated lives, but were not isolated. And they demonstrated a unity that transcended racial, social, and cultural barriers and pointed to Christ.

To discover what is involved in living for Christ like that, let's pick up our study in Philippians 3, where Paul explains how to march in step with God's grand strategy.

### We Need Examples to Follow

> Brethren, join in following my example, and observe those who walk according to the pattern you have in us. (v. 17)

Jesus told us not to be isolated from the lost, and now, through Paul, He's also telling us not to isolate ourselves from other believers. To live as salt and light in this darkened world, we need mature models in the faith such as Paul, Timothy, or Epaphroditus.

What exactly makes someone a good model to follow? Paul answers that question in his second letter to Timothy.

> But you followed my teaching, conduct, purpose, faith, patience, love, perseverance, persecutions, and sufferings. (2 Tim. 3:10–11a)

As you seek out someone to follow as Timothy did Paul, here are three practical suggestions to remember:

- Choose your mentors slowly and carefully.

- Study their lives privately.

- Follow those most worthy of your personal admiration.

### We Live among Many Who Are Enemies of the Cross

> For many walk, of whom I often told you, and now tell you even weeping, that they are enemies of the cross of Christ, whose end is destruction, whose god is their appetite, and whose glory is in their shame, who set their minds on earthly things. (Phil. 3:18–19)

Strong words, but not arrogant. The Apostle weeps as he considers the heartbreaking realities of the lost. For they are:

- *Destined for eternal hopelessness.* That is their future. An eternity without Christ means an eternity without love, joy, laughter, or anything good.

- *Driven by sensual appetites.* Since they have only themselves to please and not God, their eat-drink-and-be-merry lifestyles drive them at a frantic pace into more and more meaninglessness.

- *Dedicated to material things.* The lost live mainly by the seen, not the unseen. They seek meaning and purpose in the tangible things they can own or achieve.

Now the point of this analysis is not to judge or condemn the lost or to leave some kind of impression that Christians are better than non-Christians. Rather, it is to help us remember why God has placed us among them. Our mission is to reach out to them! To *win* them. To help them realize that there is so much more to life than they have ever known.

### We Belong to Those Who Are Bound for Heaven

> For our citizenship is in heaven, from which also we eagerly wait for a Savior, the Lord Jesus Christ; who will transform the body of our humble state into conformity with the body of His glory, by the exertion of the power that He has even to subject all things to Himself. (vv. 20–21)

To keep us from getting too attached to the things of this world, Paul reminds us that we are citizens of heaven. Remember what he said of the lost? They "set their minds on earthly things" (v. 19). As believers, however, we're to set our minds on the things above (see Col. 3:2). How? By eagerly awaiting Christ's return, by anticipating our future transformation, and by cooperating with God's Spirit to conform us into the image of His Son.

The problem for many believers is not that they're so heavenly-minded they're of no earthly good; it's that they are so earthly-minded they no longer create a hunger in others for heavenly things. We get so caught up in materialism and earthly values that the light of Christ becomes barely a flicker. The lost around us continue thirsting for the living water; they continue stumbling in the dark not knowing the way, the truth, and the life. Paul says to let our conduct be heavenly among the enemies of God on earth.

### We Must Stand Firm, but Not Stand Still

> Therefore, my beloved brethren whom I long to see, my joy and crown, so stand firm in the Lord, my beloved. (Phil. 4:1)

The common thread throughout Paul's letter to the Philippians is a focus on the Lord. He is the source of our confidence, joy, and strength to stand firm.

Remember this, however. Standing firm does not mean standing still. Living as citizens of heaven among enemies of the Cross will never be easy. The spiritual warfare is intense; we can easily panic, lose our sense of stability, and defect. We must, therefore, actively pursue a strategy of steadfastness. And that can only be accomplished through Christ's strength. Stand firm—*in the Lord!*

## A Concluding Inspection

To close, let's step back from our study and consider how well we are marching in step with God's strategy. Are you following good examples? Are you in contact with and reaching out to enemies of the Cross? Is your conduct uniquely Christian? Have you been standing firm?

God has left us here for a reason: to reach out to those who are still in the dark and bring them into the light of Christ. When you understand that, you realize His strategy isn't so strange after all. In fact, it is the most sane and loving strategy ever to be conceived or executed.

### Living Insights                                                STUDY ONE

Our citizenship is in heaven. (Phil. 3:20a)

"Here was a picture," wrote commentator William Barclay, "the Philippians could understand.

> Philippi was a Roman colony. Here and there at strategic military centers the Romans set down their colonies. In such places the citizens were mostly soldiers who had served their time—twenty-one years —and who had been rewarded with full citizenship. The great characteristic of these colonies was that, wherever they were, they remained fragments of Rome. Roman dress was worn; Roman magistrates governed; the Latin tongue was spoken; Roman justice was administered; Roman morals were observed. Even in the ends of the earth they remained unshakeably Roman. Paul says to the Philippians, "Just

as the Roman colonists never forget that they belong
to Rome, you must never forget that you are citizens
of heaven; and your conduct must match your citizenship."[2]

Think about your conduct. Does it match your citizenship? Are
you unshakeably committed to Christ even in those remote corners
of your life where no one else sees you? How about in the everyday
affairs where life is just normal, routine?

- Can the waitress at the restaurant tell by the way you treat her
  that you are a citizen of heaven?

- Can the people on the freeway tell a difference by the way you
  drive?

- Does your conduct match your citizenship behind the doors of
  your home?

- Whose morals do you observe when you're on a business trip
  alone?

- How do you treat others on the phone or at work?

"Wherever they were, they remained fragments of Rome."[3] Can
the same be said of you concerning your citizenship in heaven?

## Living Insights                                    STUDY TWO

Do you want to know what's really a strange strategy? Christians
who consciously avoid non-Christians. Ever know someone like
that? Some believers actually boast about not having pagan friends,
as if it made them more spiritual because none of their friends drank
or used profanity. In some circles, this is a real mark of maturity.

There were people with this same attitude in Jesus' day. "Why
is your Teacher eating with the tax-gatherers and sinners?" the
Pharisees complained to the disciples (Matt. 9:11). They couldn't
stand to see Him rubbing shoulders with such riffraff. It didn't make
sense. But then, they didn't understand God's strategy.

---

2. William Barclay, *The Letters to the Philippians, Colossians, and Thessalonians,* rev. ed., The
Daily Study Bible Series (Philadelphia, Pa.: Westminster Press, 1975), p. 69.

3. Barclay, *Philippians, Colossians, and Thessalonians,* p. 69.

How well do you understand God's strategy for using you to reach out to lost and hurting people? Are you afraid to touch the untouchables of society? Will you allow tax-gatherers and sinners into your home? What kind of attitude is reflected in the way you treat the lost—compassionate and understanding, or pharisaical and judgmental?

Think about which strategy you're pursuing with nonbelievers—that of the Pharisees or of Jesus?

Chapter 11

# DEFUSING DISHARMONY

*Philippians 4:1–3*

According to forest folklore, two porcupines huddled together one cold Canadian night to get warm. The closer they got, however, the more their quills kept pricking one another. Eventually, they abandoned the idea and moved apart. Separated and exposed, both began shivering; so they quickly decided to sidle up close again. When they did, each jabbed and irritated the other as before, causing them to part for a second time. This went on again and again, with always the same result. They needed each other, but they kept needling each other![1]

Christians are a lot like that. We profess to need each other, and we do, but we keep getting on each other's nerves. Why? What is it that causes Christ's church to behave more at times like a brawling tough than the gloriously spotless and holy bride Jesus is preparing for Himself? How is it that grown adults, much less Christians, can split a church right down the middle over what hymnbook to use or what color to paint the nursery?

To find out what causes our contentions, let's turn to James 4.

## Analyzing Conflict's Cause and Extent

Church squabbles aren't simply a twentieth-century malady. Believers have bickered since the church's beginning, which is what prompted the apostle James to ask in his usual direct way:

> What is the source of quarrels and conflicts among you? Is not the source your pleasures that wage war in your members? You lust and do not have; so you commit murder. And you are envious and cannot obtain; so you fight and quarrel. You do not have because you do not ask. You ask and do not receive, because you ask with wrong motives, so that you may spend it on your pleasures. (James 4:1–3)

---

1. Based on a story told in Leslie B. Flynn's book *When the Saints Come Storming In* (Wheaton, Ill.: Scripture Press Publications, Victor Books, 1988), p. 14.

James describes the disharmony in his day using two descriptive words: *quarrels* and *conflicts*. The Greek term for *quarrels* refers to widespread warfare, a theater of war like the South Pacific or Europe during World War II. *Conflicts*, on the other hand, is the term used to describe smaller skirmishes, local fights, or personal battles. Christ's body has long been a battleground, with full-scale wars as well as petty scuffles, the same as it is today.

England and Northern Ireland battle on over centuries-old territorial and denominational issues, using bombs and bullets that are only too real. Great wars of doctrine still split churches and divide denominations. Even seminaries join the fray, firing off great salvos of theological rhetoric in journals and books. Smaller-scale skirmishes also tear at the body of Christ through power struggles, arguments, envy, lawsuits, catty comments, and silent standoffs. These kinds of ugly clashes wound and maim people's spirits.

Is James implying, then, that Christians should never disagree? Must we simply strive to always preserve the appearance of peace and harmony? No, absolutely not. To compromise on convictions that are clearly set forth in Scripture achieves only uniformity, not unity. Unity allows us to disagree—yet it keeps us from being disagreeable.

What is it that makes us so intolerant, so violent over sometimes petty issues? Why do we mistreat others over matters involving nothing more than personal preference? The infighting, verbal assaults, and mean-spirited stubbornness—where does it all come from? James knows.

### Why We Have Them

"Is not the source your pleasures that wage war in your members?" he bluntly observes (v. 1). Pleasures—that doesn't sound all that evil or hostile, does it? In Greek, however, the term for this word is *hēdonē*, from which we get the word *hedonism*. James is speaking of desire without restraint, pleasure without boundaries, passion to get what one wants, regardless. That's the source of disharmony. And he adds that this raw selfishness wages war; it *strateuō*—strategizes— to get what it wants. How far will we go to get what we want?

> You lust and do not have; so you commit murder.
> And you are envious and cannot obtain; so you fight
> and quarrel. (v. 2a)

If someone gets in our way—we fight! If we need others on our side to win—we enlist! If it takes sharp, cutting words to overcome our adversaries—we murder! Not physically, perhaps, but with killing looks, slander, and gossip (see Prov. 18:21a).

## Ways We Express Our Disharmony

More often than not, quarrels and conflicts in the church manifest themselves in personal power plays, political maneuvering, strong-arm tactics, stubborn deafness, rumors, and back-biting.

In his book *Well-Intentioned Dragons*, Marshall Shelley identifies some of the people behind such disharmony. Surprisingly, they're usually folks who don't necessarily mean to be difficult but are anyway.

> Within the church, they are often sincere, well-meaning saints, but they leave ulcers, strained relationships, and hard feelings in their wake. They don't consider themselves difficult people. They don't sit up nights thinking of ways to be nasty. Often they are pillars of the community—talented, strong personalities, deservingly respected—but for some reason, they undermine the ministry of the church. They are not naturally rebellious or pathological; they are loyal church members, convinced they're serving God, but they wind up doing more harm than good.
>
> They can drive pastors crazy . . . or out of the church.
>
> Some dragons are openly critical. They are the ones who accuse you of being (pick one) too spiritual, not spiritual enough, too dominant, too laid back, too narrow, too loose, too structured, too disorganized, or ulterior in your motives. . . .
>
> Sightings of these dragons are all too common. As one veteran pastor says, "Anyone who's been in ministry more than an hour and a half knows the wrath of a dragon." Or, as Harry Ironside described it, "Wherever there's light, there's bugs."[2]

2. Marshall Shelley, *Well-Intentioned Dragons* (Waco, Tex.: Word Books, Publisher, 1985), pp. 11–12.

## Looking through the Keyhole of a Century-One Church

Let's turn our attention now from a textbook analysis of conflict's anatomy to a real-life example found in Philippians 4. Through a keyhole the size of three verses, Paul allows us to glimpse a first-century skirmish in the church at Philippi.

### A Primary Principle

Before addressing the specific conflict, Paul first calls for a return to the fundamental principle that defuses disharmony.

> Therefore, my beloved brethren whom I long to see, my joy and crown, so stand firm in the Lord, my beloved. (v. 1)

Agreeing with James that our pleasures wage war to satisfy self, Paul urges his readers to adopt a different strategy—standing firm in the Lord. It's the same strategy he mentioned earlier, in Philippians 1.

> Only conduct yourselves in a manner worthy of the gospel of Christ; so that whether I come and see you or remain absent, I may hear of you that you are *standing firm in one spirit*, with one mind striving together for the faith of the gospel. (v. 27, emphasis added)

This same principle is also found in several other of the Apostle's epistles.

> Stand firm in the faith. (1 Cor. 16:13)

> Keep standing firm. (Gal. 5:1)

> Now we really live, if you stand firm in the Lord. (1 Thess. 3:8)

> So then, brethren, stand firm. (2 Thess. 2:15)

Why did Paul continually repeat this concept? Because it is a foundational principle for maintaining harmony.

> *Standing firm in the Lord*
> *precedes*
> *relating well in the family.*

Standing firm in the Lord means following Christ's teachings, respecting His Word, modeling His priorities, loving His people, and carrying out His will. When believers commit themselves to goals such as these instead of their own selfish pursuits, they will have little difficulty relating well to other members of God's family.

### A Relational Need

Next, Paul moves from principle to people and actually names the two whose conflict was so well-known that it had even reached the Apostle's ears in distant Rome.

> I urge Euodia and I urge Syntyche to live in harmony in the Lord. (Phil. 4:2)

Even from such a brief glimpse, there are at least five important observations we can make.

1. These are two women in the Philippian church (feminine names).
2. They are mentioned nowhere else in the Scriptures.
3. The details of their dispute are not revealed.
4. Paul's counsel is to urge them toward harmony: "I urge . . . I urge" (he neither rebukes nor instructs them).
5. He appeals to their hearts (intrinsic motivation).

Did you also notice what Paul doesn't write? He doesn't spell out a step-by-step process for reconciliation. He doesn't try to take charge and tell Euodia and Syntyche what to do, as if they were children. Nor does he attempt to bully these women with a threat, "Get this thing resolved by next week, or I'll . . ." Instead, he graciously allows them the dignity of working things out on their own.

Coupled with the dignity and grace Paul packs into this one little sentence is also a deep sense of concern. Twice he uses the word *urge*, suggesting that both women were at fault in this dispute. In fact, the Latin Vulgate version of this verse uses two different verbs before the two women's names, implying again this idea of mutual wrong.

What is the common ground of agreement that Paul calls them to? "To live in harmony in the Lord" (v. 2b). The Apostle isn't asking them to hold the same opinions or agree on every jot or tittle of Scripture. He's calling them to find harmony in their common Lord and Savior. How? He's already given them the answer to that earlier in the letter. If the root cause of disputes is selfishness, then we must adopt the kind of unselfish attitude he wrote about in chapter 2.

Do nothing from selfishness or empty conceit, but with humility of mind let each of you regard one another as more important than himself; do not merely look out for your own personal interests, but also for the interests of others. Have this attitude in yourselves which was also in Christ Jesus. (vv. 3–5)

Only if these two women stop strategizing to accomplish their will and adopt Christ's attitude instead will there be any hope for harmony and reconciliation.

### An Affirming Request

Occasionally, a dispute is so deep and long-standing that it takes the help of a third party—an objective mediator—to resolve matters and restore the relationship. Paul apparently felt the conflict between Euodia and Syntyche warranted just such a person, so he asks a close friend to act as an arbitrator.

Indeed, true comrade, I ask you also to help these women who have shared my struggle in the cause of the gospel, together with Clement also, and the rest of my fellow workers, whose names are in the book of life. (4:3)

All sorts of suggestions have been made as to the identity of this "true comrade," but no one knows for sure. What's more significant is the help this person could give these two women—saints who were very important to Paul, because they had shared in his struggle for the gospel and belonged to the same spiritual family. But now they were acting like two Canadian porcupines, jabbing and irritating one another, and the situation needed resolution—soon!

## Considering the Lessons This Teaches Us

Euodia and Syntyche—they needed each other, but they kept needling each other. But let's not be too hard on them because the truth is, we've all done some needling ourselves. So instead of remembering them as just two of Christ's brides that needed to stop brawling, let them remind you of these four practical principles.

First: *Clashes will continue to occur.* So long as the raw selfishness of our sin natures wages war, conflicts will continue. There's no such thing as a conflict-free family . . . not even among God's family. Disagreements are to be expected.

Second: *Not all conflicts are wrong.* Not all disagreements call for reconciliation. Occasionally, it is right to disagree, especially when the issues concern the fundamental truths of the Scriptures and not merely personal tastes or personalities.

Third: *If the disagreement should be resolved and could be resolved, but it is not, then stubbornness and selfishness are at the core.* Though we are adults in age and height, we can be awfully childish in our attitudes.

And fourth: *Should you be the "comrade" needed to assist in the reconciliation, remember this threefold objective:*

- The ultimate goal: restoration, not discipline.

- The right attitude: grace, not force.

- The common ground: Christ, not logic, church policy, tradition, or your will.

## Living Insights

Since the title of this chapter is "Defusing Disharmony," why don't we try to do a little of that? I say "a little" simply because it's more realistic. Life's too messy to suppose that conflicts in our lives can be neatly resolved in the space of one Living Insight. So let's just try a little. Who knows, maybe for you that will end up being a lot!

To begin, think of a particular conflict you're dealing with right now, and identify the issues involved.

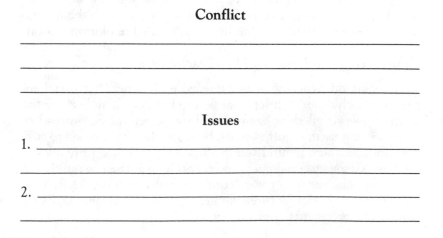

**Conflict**

_____

_____

_____

**Issues**

1. _____

_____

2. _____

_____

3. _____

_____

4. _____

_____

Now look back at the issues you've listed, and ask yourself if an eternal principle is at stake in each of these or merely a difference of opinion or taste.

Perhaps some issues do involve biblical truths that you shouldn't back down on. But it's also possible that you may be vigorously fighting over something that, when you look at it closely, represents only a personal preference. Certainly it is OK to express your opinions, but cause a split? Cause someone to get fired? Cause Christ's bride to become the laughingstock of the community over a matter that in eternity won't matter? The apostle Paul has a better plan. In Romans 12:18 he states:

> If possible, so far as it depends on you, be at peace
> with all men.

What step, however little, could you take this week to pursue peace with this other person over any issues not involving an eternal principle?

_____

_____

_____

### 🍇 *Living Insights*                                    STUDY TWO

As we noted in our lesson, not all conflicts are wrong. Sometimes it is right to disagree—just be careful *how* you do it. The way in which you disagree often determines whether a squabble will be a brief conflict, a lengthy quarrel, or the end of life as you know it!

Think back on the conflict you dealt with in the first Living Insight. Are you glorifying God with the way you're handling this situation? Is His love and humility evident in your attitude toward this other person? Can others tell that you're seeking Christ's will and not just your own?

Take some time to meditatively read the following passages: Romans 12:9–21; Matthew 5:43–48; and Luke 10:27. Once you've finished, spend some time answering these questions:

- How am I fulfilling the Great Commandment in this conflict?

  _____

  _____

- How am I not fulfilling the Great Commandment in this conflict?

  _____

  _____

The difference between disagreeing and being disagreeable is an important one. Proverbs 18:19 states:

A brother offended is harder to be won than a strong
     city,
And contentions are like the bars of a castle.

So how we disagree is important. Not only after a conflict has begun, but even before. Suppose someone wrongs you. Even then, at the moment when the injury first occurs, we can choose to respond in such a way that disharmony can be defused.

The next time you find yourself in this situation, ask yourself, Is this issue worth the risk of offending this brother or sister? Could you not, even if you have been wronged, invoke the principle in 1 Peter 4:8 about love covering a multitude of sins and graciously forgive this person without ever having to bring it up? Would you be willing to relinquish a freedom you have in Christ if it is creating a legitimate stumbling block for another brother or sister?

Your response will show how real your concern is for the unity of Christ's body.

## Chapter 12

# FREEING YOURSELF UP TO LAUGH AGAIN

*Philippians 4:4–9*

One of the most precious words in the lexicon of any language is *freedom*. We all want it, treasure it, even fight for it . . . freedom from governmental tyranny; freedom to think and express ourselves; freedom to worship as we choose; freedom to pursue our dreams unshackled from prejudice and hatred. Humankind's fiercest battles have been fought over these and other issues, all stemming from that one prized word—freedom.

## Getting Serious about Being Set Free

The idea of freedom is not the invention of any one country's constitution; rather, it is a gift of God given to the soul of every human being. How?

- He made us with minds . . . that we might think freely.

- He made us with hearts . . . that we might love freely.

- He made us with wills . . . that we might obey freely.

Instead of putting rings in our noses so He could pull us around like oxen, the Lord has given us the incredible freedom to choose our own way. Ideally, His desire for us is to choose the way, the truth, and the life that is found in His Son. Nothing brings Him more pleasure and glory than when we freely worship and obey Him.

But the downside of this wonderful gift of freedom is that we are also free to reject Him. We are free to make wrong choices that can eventually lead to a self-made prison called addiction—the utter dead end of freedom out of control.

### What God Has Promised

The curse of sinful choices is that we suffer not only awful consequences like addictions, but also enslavement. Jesus said, "Everyone who commits sin is the slave of sin" (John 8:34). And that is why God sent His Son to earth, to release us from captivity.

One of the earliest declarations of the Messiah's mission is found in Isaiah 61. In this ancient prophecy, written seven centuries before Christ's birth, Isaiah revealed the "job description" which Jesus departed from heaven to fulfill on earth.

> The Spirit of the Lord God is upon me,
> Because the Lord has anointed me
> To bring good news to the afflicted;
> He has sent me to bind up the brokenhearted,
> To proclaim liberty to captives,
> And freedom to prisoners;
> To proclaim the favorable year of the Lord.
> (vv. 1–2a)

On the surface, it appears as if Isaiah was writing about himself. Actually, however, this is but one of the many messianic sections in his book where he wrote of the Christ who was yet to come. How do we know for sure? Notice what Jesus said when He began His ministry in Nazareth.

> And He came to Nazareth, where He had been brought up; and as was His custom, He entered the synagogue on the Sabbath, and stood up to read. And the book of the prophet Isaiah was handed to Him. And He opened the book, and found the place where it was written,
> "The Spirit of the Lord is upon Me,
> Because He anointed Me to preach the
> gospel to the poor.
> He has sent Me to proclaim release to the
> captives,
> And recovery of sight to the blind,
> To set free those who are downtrodden,
> To proclaim the favorable year of the Lord."
> And He closed the book, and gave it back to the attendant, and sat down; and the eyes of all in the synagogue were fixed upon Him. And He began to say to them, "Today this Scripture has been fulfilled in your hearing." (Luke 4:16–21)

With Jesus, Isaiah's "favorable year of the Lord" had come! His mission was exactly what Isaiah had prophesied it would be— proclaiming release to the captives and setting free those who are downtrodden. Not a freedom for those behind literal bars, but for those trapped in their own self-made prisons of sin and addictions.

### How We Have Responded

The sad truth is that even though Christ has come to set us free, many of us are still enslaved to sin and continually opt for bad choices that tighten our shackles. By and large, we're still hopeless captives. As the eighteenth-century French philosopher Jean-Jacques Rousseau aptly said, "Man was born free, and everywhere he is in chains."[1]

## The Most Universal of All Addictions

Thus far we've dealt with the problem of addiction only in a generalized way. Now let's get specific and focus on the one enslaving habit that keeps nearly all of us in chains—worry.

Many of us are addicted to worry because we simply don't view it as being sinful. It's become acceptable, something we blithely excuse without a second thought. After all, it doesn't have the same obvious harmful effects that, say, alcohol or drugs do. It seems more like a normal part of the human condition. Who can imagine life without worry?

Jesus could. And the addiction to worry is the one addiction He took time to directly address.

### Analyzing the Problem

Nowhere does Christ proclaim freedom to prisoners of worry in a more concentrated way than in Matthew 6:25–34. Five times in this central passage from His Sermon on the Mount, Jesus repeats the same Greek term for anxious, *merimnaō*, which actually means "to divide, to separate."

> For this reason I say to you, do not be anxious. (v. 25)

> Which of you by being anxious can add a single cubit to his life's span? (v. 27)

> And why are you anxious about clothing? (v. 28)

> Do not be anxious then. (v. 31)

1. Jean-Jacques Rousseau, as quoted in *Bartlett's Familiar Quotations*, 15th ed., rev. and enl., ed. Emily Morison Beck (Boston, Mass.: Little, Brown and Co., 1980), p. 358.

Therefore do not be anxious for tomorrow. (v. 34)

To better understand what Jesus means by *anxious*, let's first underscore what He does not mean. He is not referring to wise foresight, a necessary sense of responsibility, or using care and thoughtfulness toward other people. Those are necessary and good qualities all Christians should exercise.

The kind of worry Jesus condemns is that which causes us to be mentally harassed and emotionally agitated, preoccupied with distressing fears, tormented, burdened about things that have not happened—but could.

From William Barclay's book *New Testament Words*, we can glean several helpful insights concerning worry. First of all, he contends that there is a "right and a wrong anxiety, a right and a wrong carefulness." On the wrong side he finds:

- The anxiety and the worry which come from too much involvement in the affairs of the world.

- Worry about the future.

- Worry that causes the expenditure of energy on nonessentials.

- Worry about how to face the oppositions and the trials which come to a Christian.

- Worry about how to please the wrong people.

The right kind of anxiety, however, looks like this:

- It is right that we should take thought for *each other.*

- It is specially right to take thought for our fellow Christians.

- It is right to take thought for the church of Christ.

"But what is forbidden is disabling worry," Barclay concludes, "and not enabling foresight."

> It is the duty of a Christian . . . to do all that he
> can and to dare all that he can and to leave the rest
> to God.[2]

God never intended His people to become prisoners to worry. Such an unbelieving, energy-draining addiction strangles our faith and makes us unable to bear fruit. But it does even more than that.

2. Condensed from William Barclay's *New Testament Words* (London, England: SCM Press, 1964), pp. 202–3.

### Identifying Its Impact

When people get hooked on worry, at least four consequences occur that can be drawn from Jesus' teaching in Matthew 6:25–34. First, our value system gets confused: "Is not life more than food, and the body than clothing?" (v. 25b). Second, we become selfish: " 'What shall *we* eat?' or 'What shall *we* drink?' or 'With what shall *we* clothe ourselves?' " (v. 31, emphasis added). Third, our Christian distinctives get blurred: "For all these things the Gentiles eagerly seek; for your heavenly Father knows that you need all these things" (v. 32). And fourth, tomorrow becomes a dread: "Therefore do not be anxious for tomorrow" (v. 34).

### Understanding God's Therapy

Now that we've identified and examined our anxiety addiction, let's look at the cure. In Philippians 4, Paul reveals God's way of freeing us from the habit of worry.

> Be anxious for nothing, but in everything by prayer
> and supplication with thanksgiving let your requests
> be made known to God. (v. 6)

Basically, God's rehab program for worriers can be summed up in six therapeutic words:

> *Worry about nothing,*
> *Pray about everything.*[3]

Remember that. Write it down on a card and place it on your bathroom mirror, in your car, on your desk, wherever you're bound to see it regularly. Let it be a constant reminder to stop worrying about the things you can't change or control and start praying about them instead. Turn your worry list into a prayer list, and commit each one of those issues that agitate, frighten, or burden you into God's hands.

Once you begin practicing God's plan for curing worry, you'll soon discover that you have time . . . lots of it. Why? Because you used to spend all that time worrying. Now it's yours again to put to good use. So what does Paul suggest you do with all that extra time?

---

3. Charles R. Swindoll, *Laugh Again* (Dallas, Tex.: Word Books, 1992), p. 199.

*Rejoice* (v. 4)
*Relax* (v. 5)
*Rest* (v. 7)

Let's take a closer look at those three beneficial time-fillers. First: Rejoice!

> Rejoice in the Lord always; again I will say, rejoice! (v. 4)

This is a command no less emphatic than the one that reads: "Worry about nothing." We're to look for the things that help us enjoy life. Find the bright side; loosen up and laugh freely; replace that frumpy old frown with a winsome smile.

Sure, at times we all experience circumstances that aren't enjoyable. Even so, there are always plenty of things to be joyful about in the Lord. Choose joy by remembering Him and His goodness. See it in creation, in another person, a song, or a kind word. If we choose instead to worry and focus only on the negative, we will miss all those things that He has put around us to give us joy.

Solomon wrote, "A joyful heart is good medicine," and, "A cheerful heart has a continual feast" (Prov. 17:22a; 15:15b). You want to have that kind of heart? Then the mandate is clear—rejoice!

Second: Relax!

> Let your forbearing spirit be known to all men. The Lord is near. (Phil. 8:5)

Where is the idea of relaxing in Paul's statement? "Forbearing spirit" is the key. It means "gentle . . . easy"; or as some would say, easygoing. Another way of putting it would be "sweet reasonableness," the opposite of a dogmatic and harsh spirit that demands and dominates. A good example would be Jesus with the woman taken in adultery. When the legalists said, "Stone her!", He forgave her (John 8:1–11). Or Paul, who said, when some preached Christ out of selfish ambition thinking it would cause him distress while imprisoned, "Christ is being proclaimed—I rejoice!" (Phil. 1:18).

Instead of worrying over every jot and tittle in everyone else's life, learn to relax. Yield a little; to those who are struggling, extend a helping hand of grace rather than a slap of condemnation. Quit trying to control everyone and everything all the time, and allow God to work in His way and in His timing—relax!

And third: Rest!

> Be anxious for nothing, but in everything by prayer and supplication with thanksgiving let your requests be made known to God. And the peace of God, which surpasses all comprehension, shall guard your hearts and your minds in Christ Jesus. (4:6–7)

Try reading this verse a second time—this time from the Living Bible, which brings the idea of resting closer to the surface.

> Don't worry about anything; instead, pray about everything; tell God your needs and don't forget to thank him for his answers. If you do this you will experience God's peace, which is far more wonderful than the human mind can understand. His peace will keep your thoughts and your hearts quiet and at rest as you trust in Christ Jesus.

In place of living uptight and uneasy lives, we can rest in God's peace. Paul describes that peace as a "guard," using a military term for marching sentry duty around something valuable or strategic. When we transfer our troubles to the Lord through prayer, we're given a silent sentry called peace to protect our minds and our emotions.

### Correcting Our Perspective

As with all addictions, worry doesn't go away just because we break the habit. It is always there, tempting, pushing, urging us to try it again. So what can we do to protect ourselves from becoming enslaved to anxiety again? Here are three crucial exercises to help you stay free.

1. *Feed your mind positive thoughts.*

> Finally, brethren, whatever is true, whatever is honorable, whatever is right, whatever is pure, whatever is lovely, whatever is of good repute, if there is any excellence and if anything worthy of praise, let your mind dwell on these things. (v. 8)

No matter what you're dealing with or how bad things get or why God may be permitting them, deliberately keep your mind focused on positive, praiseworthy ideas. Worry will starve on such food for thought. So refuse to ruminate on negative junk foods like shame, fear, or guilt, which strengthen worry and strangle peace.

2. *Focus your attention on encouraging models.*

> The things you have learned and received and heard
> and seen in me, practice these things. (v. 9a)

Whenever the Philippians needed their faith encouraged, all they had to do was look to Paul. For them, he provided a wealth of things to be learned, received, heard, and seen—things that would strengthen them to continue. Is there someone like that for you? Someone whose life motivates you to grow and persevere? If you can't find anyone close to you, perhaps an inspiring biography would meet this need.

3. *Find "the God of peace" in every circumstance.*

> And the God of peace shall be with you. (v. 9b)

Worry not only steals our joy, it also blinds us to God's peace. It forces us to focus on the wrong things. As recovering anxiety addicts, we must always remember to give our mental burdens to the Lord in every circumstance. Only then will our eyes be opened to find God's peace.

## Finding Hope Beyond an Old Habit

The wonderful hope for worry addicts is Jesus Christ. As Isaiah said, He comes to bind up the brokenhearted, to proclaim liberty to captives and freedom to prisoners—and that includes prisoners of worry. The only trouble is, we've got the freedom to accept Him or reject Him. We can elect to stay in our self-made cells and fret, or we can walk out and have life and have it more abundantly. The door is open. Which will you choose?

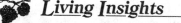 *Living Insights* STUDY ONE

Open any letter shared between good friends, and you'll likely read something similar to this honest-to-goodness, let-me-tell-you-how-I-feel excerpt.

Dear —

My life stinks! How's the family? I'm OK — really I am — but don't touch me or I'll have to kill you.

As you can probably tell from the preceding, everything is pretty normal around here. The central air in our house doesn't work; the car is hanging on, having only required a $250 clutch/brake job; the washing machine fell apart; the hard drive on my PC crashed (and burned); the door fell off the dishwasher; and we have a hot water leak (you can hear it running, but we can't find it). That is just in the last month. We have other exciting stories dealing mostly with money that I won't bore you with. I know someone's bound to have it worse than me (I pity da fool!), but occasionally I think Job had it easy.

Today I decided to write down a list of things that are causing me stress, thinking that if I got them down on paper they may not seem so bad. . . . I quit at #17; it stressed me out!

"Everything is pretty normal around here." Normal meaning full, stretched, uncertain, not enough, broken, unexpected, and frustrating. That's normal. That's the kind of daily bread life hands us.

Are things pretty "normal" where you live? Probably. Is it stressing you out? When you reach into your mind for something good to dwell on, are the cupboards empty?

Instead of writing down the things that are causing you stress, why not restock your thoughts using the grocery list Paul recommends in Philippians 4:8? Work your way down the list, giving at least two specific examples for each item.

True: _____

_____

Honorable: _____

_____

Right: _____

_____

Pure: _____

_____

Lovely: _____

_____

Of Good Repute: _____

_____

Excellent: _____

_____

Worthy of Praise: _____

_____

Now that's the kind of daily bread your Heavenly Father wants you to be nourished on. So if you want a taste of joy, let your mind chew on those things—not that "normal" stuff life dishes out that can cause nothing but upset stomachs, headaches, and ulcers.

We worry, we complain, we vent our frustrations, we become depressed, we recite our troubles to others around us . . .

. . . but the problem never gets resolved.

Not really. Oh, we may experience a momentary catharsis at times by sharing our pain with close friends, but then it just comes back, stronger, more deeply rooted than before. Which drives us back to those same friends for a second and third time to recount more of the same sad tale.

"Lord, why aren't You helping me?" we wonder as the situation gets worse instead of better. So we seek out more people to empathize with us as we talk about our problem which, by now, is causing a lot of problems. We talk a lot about the Lord, too, hours on end talking, talking, talking—but nothing seems to help. Nothing changes.

Why? What is it that we're missing? What is it that we're doing that keeps defeating us? We're talking but never praying. We spend all our time bringing our hurts and frustrations just to our friends instead of to the Lord as well. Not that He can't use our friends to help us, but going to them is no substitute for coming to Him. In fact, going to our friends can become a subtle way of avoiding the Father and actually dealing with the problem. We say we're seeking help, when what we're really seeking is another opportunity to vent our anger at the person who has hurt us and gain a little more sympathy.

Could this be happening to you? Is there a particularly worrisome situation in your life right now? How many times already have you talked it out with friends? How about the Lord? Have you been as honest about your pain, desire, and need with God as you have been with your best friend?

We rarely are. But today, right now, why not pause and commit yourself to following Paul's advice in Philippians 4:6:

> Be anxious for nothing, but in everything by prayer
> and supplication with thanksgiving let your requests
> be made known to God.

Make yourself "known to God," not just to your friends. Take your concern to Him, for as one writer put it, "There is nothing too great for God's power; and nothing too small for His fatherly care."[4]

---

4. William Barclay, *The Letters to the Philippians, Colossians, and Thessalonians*, rev. ed., The Daily Study Bible Series (Philadelphia, Pa.: Westminster Press, 1975), p. 77.

## Chapter 13

# DON'T FORGET TO HAVE FUN AS YOU GROW UP

*Philippians 4:10–19*

Today, staying young has become a national obsession. Wrinkles are out and face-lifts are in. Tummy tucks are popular too. So are hair transplants, implants, liposuction, aerobics, revitalizing creams—even chin straps. That's right, people wear them at night to train up sagging skin. But do what we will to our bodies, nothing can guard us from getting older. It's one of those involuntary realities that, like it or not, ready or not, here it comes!

Age is a matter of fact. Maturity, on the other hand, is a matter of choice. If we really want to be preoccupied about something, the Scriptures recommend focusing on growing up, not growing old.

> We are no longer to be children, tossed here and there by waves, and carried about by every wind of doctrine, by the trickery of men, by craftiness in deceitful scheming; but speaking the truth in love, we are to grow up in all aspects into Him, who is the head, even Christ. (Eph. 4:14–15)

> Therefore, putting aside all malice and all guile and hypocrisy and envy and all slander, like newborn babes, long for the pure milk of the word, that by it you may grow in respect to salvation. (1 Pet. 2:1–2)

> But solid food is for the mature, who because of practice have their senses trained to discern good and evil. Therefore leaving the elementary teaching about the Christ, let us press on to maturity. (Heb. 5:14–6:1a)

God's goal for His people is growth, so pressing on toward maturity is our challenge. Though growing older may be automatic, growing up is something we must accomplish choice by choice.

## That Elusive Quality of Maturity

Since our major challenge in life is not age but maturity, let's uncover the seldom-mined riches of this trait.

### Exactly What Is It?

Maturity is the process of leaving behind childish habits and consistently moving toward emotional and spiritual adulthood. It's being responsible for one's own decisions, motives, actions, and their consequences. Maturity doesn't happen overnight or in a single decision, but grows over a lifetime as we pay attention to how we are living and learn how to change. The more we strive for it, the more our lives become marked by stability and balance.

### How Is It Expressed?

Maturity manifests itself in many ways. Such as . . .

- When we are as concerned for others as for ourselves.

- When the presence of danger or evil is discerned before it becomes obvious.

- When disagreements can be expressed without being disagreeable.

- When knowledge is transformed into wisdom.

- When high ideals are accompanied by the discipline of action.

- When compassion and involvement match an awareness of need.

- When there is determination to stay committed to the task.

- When spiritual growth is pursued privately as well as corporately in the church.

- When there is a willingness to change once we are convinced that correction is in order.

- When . . .

We could all add more traits. For a closer look at how maturity is expressed, however, let's go beyond our list and examine a life.

## Two Sides of the Same Quality

In Philippians 4, we'll find maturity on display not only in the life of the apostle Paul but also in the lives of the people to whom he wrote.

### Maturity of Paul

As we begin our study with verses 10–13, no less than four characteristics of maturity emerge in Paul's life.

First: He is affirming.

> But I rejoiced in the Lord greatly, that now at
> last you have revived your concern for me; indeed,
> you were concerned before, but you lacked oppor-
> tunity. (v. 10)

By saying that the Philippians had revived their concern for him, Paul means they had sent another contribution to help him press on. Since the day he left ten years earlier, the church at Philippi had continued to be concerned about the Apostle's welfare and ministry. Apparently, they had wanted to demonstrate their devotion to him before by sending an offering, but they "lacked opportunity"—meaning they either didn't know his whereabouts or they had no way to get it to him.

Normally, it is the other way around for many people—they have the opportunity, but they lack concern. Not so with the Philippians. And Paul affirms them for this, which is a true mark of his maturity. The Apostle says in effect, "Even when I didn't hear from you, I knew that you were concerned for me." Paul thought the best of others. He upheld their intentions, never doubting that they cared.

Second: He is contented.

> Not that I speak from want; for I have learned to
> be content in whatever circumstances I am. (v. 11)

Maturity is never more evident than when someone possesses the quality of contentment. And no one modeled this particular trait better than Paul. He wouldn't allow circumstances to control his attitude. Not prison, not the possibility of death, not chains, not whether the Philippians had sent a gift, nothing. Regardless of the winds that blew, he could find contentment in Christ.

Many people are like thermometers—they merely register whatever the climate is around them. If the pressure is high and things are tense, they're tight and irritable. If life is stormy, they become worried and afraid. If things are calm and relaxed, they read peaceful and quiet. Others, though, resemble Paul. They're more regulated and consistent, like thermostats, maintaining a mature attitude in spite of life's highs and lows.

But does this mean Paul simply didn't care what happened around him? Is that what contentment is—indifference? No. The Greek term Paul uses here suggests "self-sufficient." In the context of this letter, it means being at peace in Christ's sufficiency. Paul could endure any situation because he was convinced that Christ was present in the midst of his every day. With Him by his side, nothing was unbearable or out of control for Paul.

Now some of you may be thinking, "I wish I had the gift of contentment like that." But wait; it's not a gift. Paul states that he *learned* to be content. He wasn't born with this ability. None of us are. The ability to accept and adapt has to be developed over time through a growing trust in Christ.

Third: He is flexible.

> I know how to get along with humble means, and I also know how to live in prosperity; in any and every circumstance I have learned the secret of being filled and going hungry, both of having abundance and suffering need. (v. 12)

If we were to chart this verse, the ups and downs of Paul's experiences would look something like this:[1]

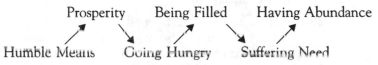

Life for Paul was a roller coaster experience. At any given time he might be riding along in humble means and in the next ascending to heights of prosperity, then plunging down into hunger, curving back up into being filled, diving into suffering need, shooting up into having abundance. Makes you dizzy! Through it all, Paul had to remain flexible. He didn't lose faith when he slept on the hard ground with a growling stomach, nor did he forget God when he had a nice home and hot meals to enjoy. Mature men and women know how to handle both situations without letting either upset their equilibrium with Christ.

And fourth: He is confident.

> I can do all things through Him who strengthens me. (v. 13)

Again, Paul confirms what we said earlier—that his sufficiency comes from a confidence in Christ's sufficiency. By pouring His power into the Apostle, Jesus enabled Paul to face or accept anything.

---

1. Charles R. Swindoll, *Laugh Again* (Dallas, Tex.: Word Books, 1992), p. 218.

And the secret of Paul's confidence can be ours as well. Only through Him can we do all things. For Paul never said:

"I can do all things through education."
"I can do all things through money."
"I can do all things through power."
"I can do all things through positive imaging."
"I can do all things through confidence in myself."

No. Nothing else suffices like Christ. He alone has the power to provide us with the strength we need.

Since we can do all things through Christ, does that mean, then, that we don't need others? On the contrary, Paul goes on to show how God used the Philippians to minister to him in his need.

### Maturity of the Philippians

By mentioning the Philippians' care and concern, Paul also reveals three traits of maturity in their lives.

First: Personal compassion.

> Nevertheless, you have done well to share with me in my affliction. And you yourselves also know, Philippians, that at the first preaching of the gospel, after I departed from Macedonia, no church shared with me in the matter of giving and receiving but you alone. (vv. 14–15)

The Philippians never forgot Paul. Once he left their city, they spontaneously and generously gave to meet his needs as he traveled in his missionary journeys. No other church demonstrated such a personal commitment to him. When the Apostle suffered, they suffered. When he was needy, they sent gifts to meet his need. When he was unable to stay in touch, they remained faithful and prayed for him. When he was arrested and imprisoned, they sent a friend to minister to him. Nothing could be more personal or compassionate.

Second: Financial generosity.

> For even in Thessalonica you sent a gift more than once for my needs. Not that I seek the gift itself, but I seek for the profit which increases to your account. (vv. 16–17)

Why does Paul say "even in Thessalonica"? He's emphasizing the generosity of the Philippians. How? Thessalonica was a wealthier city than Philippi. Nevertheless, the Philippians continued to send gifts—more than once! Their generosity simply overflowed. To such mature individuals as the Philippians, things like which city the Apostle was staying in or who had the most money didn't matter. Supporting Paul was all that mattered. And to that end, they gave generously.

Notice, too, what excited Paul about their gifts. It wasn't the gifts themselves—sure, he needed them to continue—but there was something more important. Paul was encouraged by the maturity perfected in the Philippians as they gave freely to support the spread of the gospel.

And third: Sacrificial commitment.

> But I have received everything in full, and have an
> abundance; I am amply supplied, having received from
> Epaphroditus what you have sent, a fragrant aroma,
> an acceptable sacrifice, well-pleasing to God. (v. 18)

Thanks to the Philippians' sacrificial commitment, Paul's needs were "amply supplied." He had more than enough. And he praises their personal compassion, financial generosity, and sacrificial commitment, describing it as "a fragrant aroma" that pleases God.

Bursting with joy and gratitude for the way God had met his needs through the Philippians, Paul then encourages them with the magnificent promise,

> And my God shall supply all your needs according
> to His riches in glory in Christ Jesus. (v. 19)

"My God . . . your needs . . . His riches . . ." Paul had seen those three ingredients blend together beautifully in his own life and was confident that God would do the same for His beloved Philippians.

## Making Maturity a Personal Matter

How can you develop the marks of maturity evidenced by Paul and the Philippians? Here are three places to look in your life that will enable you to grow up instead of just growing old.

1. *Look within . . . and release.* Is there something inside, in your heart, that's stunting your growth? Something other than Christ that you're tightly hanging on to? Let it go. Release it, and learn to hold tightly to Him instead. You may feel scared, weak, unable; but just remember what the Lord promised through Paul: "I can do all things through Him who strengthens me" (v. 13).

111

2. *Look around . . . and respond.* Don't wait for someone else—act on your own. The Philippians saw Paul's needs and responded. They didn't wait for another church to act first, nor did they hold back from responding a second time until someone else followed their example. They gave and continued to give without hesitation. When God shows you a need, don't wait—respond!

3. *Look up . . . and rejoice.* Take time to look up and survey all that God has done for you. Consider the riches He has provided through His Son. Rejoice in every good thing bestowed and every perfect gift from above that comes from the Father of lights (see James 1:17). And then be willing to rejoice over the good things God accomplishes in the lives of others, as Paul did with the Philippians and they with him.

## Concluding Thought

In her book *Afternoon,* Jeanne Hendricks writes:

> Living is not a spectator sport. No one, at any price, is privileged to sit in the stands and watch the action from a distance. Being born means being a participant in the arena of life, where opposition is fierce and winning comes only to those who exert every ounce of energy.[2]

The same is true of growing up as we grow older. Maturity is not a spectator sport. It comes only to those who exert every ounce of energy in this arena we call life. Unlike living, however, with maturity we do have a choice. We can sit in the stands and grow old watching the action from a distance, or we can jump onto the field and strive to grow up.

Are you choosing to be a player?

## Living Insights                                         STUDY ONE

Let's devote our time here to making maturity more of a personal matter. Using the second practical application from our lesson, *look around . . . and respond,* ask yourself if there is a Paul in your life, someone who's reaching out to others with the gospel and in need

---

2. Jeanne Hendricks, *Afternoon* (Nashville, Tenn.: Thomas Nelson Publishers, 1979), p. 103.

of support. Spend the next few minutes looking around at the various needs this person might have, and write down all that come to mind—regardless of whether you feel you could meet them. (If you're short on ideas, look again at the different needs the Philippians found in Paul.)

## Look Around

_____    _____

_____    _____

_____    _____

Next, go back over this list and select at least one, if not two, needs that you can respond to this week. Perhaps there's something you can give . . . time, money, a written word of encouragement? Maybe you can't meet a specific need, but you know someone who could. Make a call and arrange a contact.

## Respond

_____

_____

_____

🍇 _Living Insights_                                  STUDY TWO

In a parable recorded in Luke 14, Jesus provides us with yet another way we can look around . . . and respond.

> "When you give a luncheon or a dinner, do not invite your friends or your brothers or your relatives or rich neighbors, lest they also invite you in return, and repayment come to you. But when you give a reception, invite the poor, the crippled, the lame, the blind, and you will be blessed, since they do not have the means to repay you; for you will be repaid at the resurrection of the righteous." (vv. 12–14)

This time, look around at the specific needs of the poor, the crippled, the lame, and the blind who live in your neighborhood, attend your church, struggle to survive in your city or in a Third World country.

## Look Around

_____     _____

_____     _____

_____     _____


Once you have a list, accept Christ's challenge and figure out how you can respond to at least two of the needs you listed.

## Respond

_____

_____

_____

_____

_____

_____

_____

## Chapter 14

# A JOYFUL, GRACE-FILLED GOOD-BYE

*Philippians 4:19–23*

Did you ever see the cartoon of the freckle-faced, Dennis-the-Menace-type toddler standing outside his parents' bedroom door? His pajama bottoms are unsnapped; his Pampers are soaked and sagging; his teddy bear's nose is torn off, and its one remaining button eye is dangling. From the looks of things, this child could definitely keep six healthy adults hopping. But in front of him, hanging from the doorknob, is the sign his exhausted mother has printed:

> CLOSED FOR BUSINESS
> MOTHERHOOD OUT OF ORDER!

Coming into this study of Philippians, many of you may have felt like that parent in the cartoon. "Closed for business. I'm out of order." Life was coming unsnapped, and your spirit was sagging.

Since then, however, Paul has taught you how to set your sails for joy, how to navigate through life's circumstances with an unsinkable confidence and contentment in Christ. Now you have an idea, along with the otters, how to take life by the throat, how to live every dip, swirl, slide down a mud bank to the fullest!

It's been an incredible letter, hasn't it? Just a few more well-chosen words and it's over. But before we enter into Paul's tender conclusion, let's turn around and take one brief look back at where we've been.

## Where Have We Been?

In chapter 1, remember, Paul revealed his *joy in living*, saying, "For me to live is Christ" (v. 21a). So long as Christ is central in our lives, nothing can steal the joy He brings.

In chapter 2, we learned from Christ's example that there could be *joy in serving*. He gave up the splendor of heaven to humble Himself on earth to the point of death on a cross. We, too, should have that same spirit of humility and selflessness, which exalts Christ and brings great glory to God the Father (vv. 5–11).

In chapter 3, Paul exhibited a *joy in sharing* his life and his ultimate goal to press on toward "the upward call of God in Christ Jesus" (v. 14). What a joy it is to realize that Christ, our loving Savior, is our ultimate goal too!

In our final chapter, we have discovered there is a *joy in resting* because Christ is our contentment. Our sufficiency comes from a confidence in Christ's sufficiency. Through the pouring of His power into us, we are able to face anything.

So many wonderful truths fill this little letter. What are some of the most memorable passages we can take with us?

## What Seems Most Memorable?

Paul's letter fairly drips with the fragrance of Christ's presence and joy. It can be seen, for example, in the letter's theme.

### The Recurring Theme

Tightly woven into Paul's theme are the words *joy* and its derivative *rejoice*, as well as many references to Jesus. The latter is mentioned over forty times, while the former is used sixteen times. Carefully stitched together under the Holy Spirit's supervision, the clear message that emerges is this: Christ is the reason for joy.

### The Major Statements

Christ is also visible in the major statements Paul makes throughout Philippians. If we were to make a scrapbook of these memorable verses, it would include passages from chapter 1, like:

> For I am confident of this very thing, that He who began a good work in you will perfect it until the day of Christ Jesus. (v. 6)

> Now I want you to know, brethren, that my circumstances have turned out for the greater progress of the gospel, so that my imprisonment in the cause of Christ has become well known throughout the whole praetorian guard and to everyone else, and that most of the brethren, trusting in the Lord because of my imprisonment, have far more courage to speak the word of God without fear. (vv. 12–14)

> For to me, to live is Christ, and to die is gain. (v. 21)

In chapter 2 we have the most concise yet comprehensive statement of Jesus' humiliation and exaltation in all the Bible.

> Have this attitude in yourselves which was also in Christ Jesus, who, although He existed in the form of God, did not regard equality with God a thing to be grasped, but emptied Himself, taking the form of a bond-servant, and being made in the likeness of men. And being found in appearance as a man, He humbled Himself by becoming obedient to the point of death, even death on a cross. Therefore also God highly exalted Him, and bestowed on Him the name which is above every name, that at the name of Jesus every knee should bow, of those who are in heaven, and on earth, and under the earth, and that every tongue should confess that Jesus Christ is Lord, to the glory of God the Father. (vv. 5–11)

Chapter 3 gives us Paul's consuming goal.

> Not that I have already obtained it, or have already become perfect, but I press on in order that I may lay hold of that for which also I was laid hold of by Christ Jesus. Brethren, I do not regard myself as having laid hold of it yet; but one thing I do: forgetting what lies behind and reaching forward to what lies ahead, I press on toward the goal for the prize of the upward call of God in Christ Jesus. (vv. 12–14)

And last, from chapter 4 come two oft-quoted statements in practically every believer's vocabulary.

> For I have learned to be content in whatever circumstances I am. I know how to get along with humble means, and I also know how to live in prosperity; in any and every circumstance I have learned the secret of being filled and going hungry, both of having abundance and suffering need. I can do all things through Him who strengthens me. (vv. 11b–13)

> And my God shall supply all your needs according to His riches in glory in Christ Jesus. (v. 19)

### The Practical Advice

As we mentioned before, Philippians is only 104 verses long. And yet some of the most practical and widely known admonitions found in the New Testament are tucked away in this brief letter. Exhortations such as:

> Only conduct yourselves in a manner worthy of the gospel of Christ; so that whether I come and see you or remain absent, I may hear of you that you are standing firm in one spirit, with one mind striving together for the faith of the gospel. (1:27)

> Do nothing from selfishness or empty conceit, but with humility of mind let each of you regard one another as more important than himself; do not merely look out for your own personal interests, but also for the interests of others. (2:3–4)

> I press on toward the goal for the prize of the upward call of God in Christ Jesus. (3:14)

> Rejoice in the Lord always; again I will say, rejoice! Let your forbearing spirit be known to all men. The Lord is near. Be anxious for nothing, but in everything by prayer and supplication with thanksgiving let your requests be made known to God. And the peace of God, which surpasses all comprehension, shall guard your hearts and your minds in Christ Jesus. Finally, brethren, whatever is true, whatever is honorable, whatever is right, whatever is pure, whatever is lovely, whatever is of good repute, if there is any excellence and if anything worthy of praise, let your mind dwell on these things. (4:4–8)

## How Do We Proceed?

The sad thing about great letters is that they end. You want so much for your friend to tell you more, to answer more questions, to stay with you a little longer. Could the Philippians not have felt this way as they came to the close of this brief letter from their beloved Paul? Tears may well have flowed from the eyes of the aged Apostle as he wrote this good-bye, as well as from the Philippians when they read it.

> And my God shall supply all your needs according to His riches in glory in Christ Jesus. Now to our God and Father be the glory forever and ever. Amen.

Greet every saint in Christ Jesus. The brethren who are with me greet you. All the saints greet you, especially those of Caesar's household.

The grace of the Lord Jesus Christ be with your spirit. (4:19–23)

Four statements for us to remember stand out in this tender farewell.

## The Glory of the Lord's Plan

In Greek, the term for *glory* Paul uses in verses 19–20 is *doxa*, which has several different meanings depending on the context. For example, it could mean brightness, splendor, and radiance, as in the glory that shone in the Holy of Holies described in the Old Testament. Or it could refer to fame, renown, or honor—in other words, that which accompanies greatness—as in, "He deserves the glory." This infers "the credit, the place of significance." From the context of Paul's closing, it appears that he has the latter meaning in mind.

In whatever circumstance—promotion or demotion, sickness or health, triumph or tragedy—we're to glorify God. Only then, when we seek to honor Him instead of ourselves in all that we do, will we experience the joy of the Lord evidenced in Paul.

## The Greeting of the Saints

The greetings Paul exchanges are easily understood, but for centuries imaginations have been spurred by his intriguing reference to "Caesar's household" (see vv. 21–22). Was he referring to the Emperor's wife? Immediate family? In-laws? Distant relatives?

The most reliable scholarship suggests that this phrase refers to an incredibly large body of Christian people in the Emperor's service in Italy and the surrounding provinces, slaves and free people alike . . . everyone from elite persons of high rank and power to the lowest slaves and common courtiers in and around the royal palace. The message of Jesus Christ flourished right under the nose of its archenemy—Nero. According to commentator Alfred Plummer,

> There is little doubt that Christianity had entered the Imperial household before St. Paul reached Rome. There were many Jews among the lower officials in Nero's household, and it was perhaps among them that the Gospel made its first converts.[1]

1. Alfred Plummer, *A Commentary on St. Paul's Epistle to the Philippians* (London, England: Robert Scott, 1919), p. 107.

No doubt, many of the believers employed in the Emperor's service had come to visit Paul. They were the faithful band that sent their greetings.

### The Grace of the Savior

Doctrinally, grace was perhaps Paul's favorite theme (v. 23). The Law had come by Moses, but grace came through Jesus Christ. He freed us from sin and provided us with the power to live obediently, in newness of life. He brought us back home to the Father, to joy. Paul is encouraging his readers to let the hope of their eternal salvation lift their spirit.

### The God of Our Lives

A brief survey of Philippians 4 alone reveals that God's pervading presence covers every second of our existence. For example,

- We're to stand firm in Him (v. 1).

- We're to find our source of joy in Him (v. 4).

- We're to let our requests be made known to Him (v. 6).

- We're to receive His peace (v. 7).

- If we follow Paul's Christlike example, the God of peace will be with us (v. 9).

- We can "do all things" through His power (v. 13).

- He is pleased with our gifts for His work (v. 18).

- It is God who supplies all our needs (v. 19).

- To Him goes all the glory forever and ever (v. 20).

God never leaves us. Even in death He is there to escort us into His glorious presence, where we will enjoy Him forever.

Having concluded his letter, perhaps the aging Apostle stood, and with the Roman guard chained to his wrist, reached over and hugged Epaphroditus. Another joyful, grace-filled good-bye took place as Paul handed him the letter he would faithfully deliver back home to Philippi and to the rest of the world.

As we part at the close of our study together, we send our warmth and affection to you, the reader, and bid you the same joyful, grace-filled good-bye.

![grapes icon] *Living Insights* STUDY ONE

Sometimes life simply refuses to cooperate; it goes in reverse instead of forward. And the more you try to correct it, the worse it becomes.

A fellow by the name of R. D. Jones had this happen to him once. The problem he encountered, however, wasn't some life-threatening situation. His house didn't burn down, he didn't fall off a cliff, nor did his car blow up while being swallowed whole in an earthquake. No, the disaster that undid him was a typographical error that went from bad to worse in a small-town newspaper.

MONDAY: For Sale—R. D. Jones has one sewing machine for sale. Phone 948-0707 after 7 p.m. and ask for Mrs. Kelly who lives with him cheap.

TUESDAY: Notice—We regret having erred in R. D. Jones' ad yesterday. It should have read, "One sewing machine for sale cheap. Phone 948-0707 and ask for Mrs. Kelly who lives with him after 7 p.m."

WEDNESDAY: Notice—R. D. Jones has informed us that he has received several annoying telephone calls because of the error we made in his classified ad yesterday. The ad stands correct as follows:
"For Sale—R.D. Jones has one sewing machine for sale. Cheap. Phone 948-0707 after 7 p.m. and ask for Mrs. Kelly who loves with him."

THURSDAY: Notice—I, R. D. Jones have no sewing machine for sale. I smashed it. Don't call 948-0707 as the telephone has been out. I have not been carrying on with Mrs. Kelly. Until yesterday she was my housekeeper but she quit. [2]

Incredible, isn't it? You can't help but laugh. The unbelievable coincidence of consecutive typos is hilarious. It's something you can't wait to tell the first friend you see. But, of course, that's only because it didn't happen to you and no one was really hurt. At times, however, life gets seriously fouled up and things like your

2. As quoted by Abigail Van Buren, *The Best of Dear Abby* (Kansas City, Mo.: Andrews and McMeel, 1981), pp. 246–47.

121

health, your finances, or your marriage go from bad, to worse, to worse than you ever thought possible.

What do you do? Paul says to give God the glory. Sounds strange, doesn't it? How do you give God the glory for disaster? Well, you don't, actually. But you do give Him glory in the way you respond to adversity. Even in the darkest moments, your life, your attitude can glorify the Lord.

Are you in the midst of a particular difficulty right now? In what specific ways are you glorifying God by your response?

_____

_____

_____

What attitude or action, if any, needs changing? Is it possible you're taking out your frustrations on your spouse, your friends, the waitress in the restaurant? Are you pretending everything is fine to avoid dealing with the problem? Are you unable to worship and trust God because you can't figure out why this has happened?

_____

_____

_____

This week, what one particular area of your life can you commit to working on?

_____

_____

## 🍇 *Living Insights*               STUDY TWO

As you look back on your study of Philippians, what seems most memorable to you?

Set aside some time to record any truths or insights you may have gained from this study that were especially significant to you.

_____

_____

# BOOKS FOR PROBING FURTHER

To learn more about Paul's letter to the Philippians and the life of joy we have with Christ, we recommend the following resources.

Briscoe, Stuart. *Bound for Joy: Philippians—Paul's Letter from Prison.* A Bible Commentary for Laymen series. Ventura, Calif.: Regal Books, 1984.

Hendriksen, William. *Philippians, Colossians, and Philemon.* New Testament Commentary series. Grand Rapids, Mich.: Baker Book House, 1979.

Lightfoot, J. B. *Commentaries on Galatians, Philippians, Colossians, and Philemon.* 3 vols. Peabody, Mass.: Hendrickson Publishers, 1981.

Swindoll, Luci. *Celebrating Life!: Catching the Thieves That Steal Your Joy.* Colorado Springs, Colo.: NavPress, 1989.

Wiersbe, Warren W. *Be Joyful.* Wheaton, Ill.: SP Publications, Victor Books, 1974.

Wirt, Sherwood Eliot. *Jesus: Man of Joy.* San Bernardino, Calif.: Here's Life Publishers, 1991.

Some of the books listed here may be out of print and available only through a library. All of these works are recommended reading only. With the exception of books by Charles R. Swindoll, none of them are available through Insight for Living. If you wish to obtain some of these suggested readings, please contact your local Christian bookstore.

# ORDERING INFORMATION

## Cassette Tapes and Study Guide

This Bible study guide was designed to be used independently or in conjunction with the broadcast of Chuck Swindoll's taped messages on the topic listed below. If you would like to order cassette tapes or further copies of this study guide, please see the information given below and the Order Forms provided at the end of this guide.

### LAUGH AGAIN

Joy. You don't see it very often nowadays. It's certainly not in the newspapers or nightly news. It's not even in many churches. Have you noticed the looks on the average Sunday morning crowd? One word comes to mind—grim. Rows of overcast faces forecast dreary to mildly depressing days, with little or no chance of any laughter.

Have the pressures of life dulled your joy in the Lord? Has your laughter become lackluster? How can your Christianity become alive and vibrant again?

Paul answers this question in a simple yet profound letter written to the Christians in Philippi. From start to finish, the outrageous joy and encouragement Paul poured out to those believers surely made them smile. And this letter still has the power to teach us how to smile, how to hold on to joy through life's storms, yes, even how to laugh again!

|         |      |                                            | Calif.* | U.S.   | B.C.*  | Canada* |
|---------|------|--------------------------------------------|---------|--------|--------|---------|
| LAF     | CS   | Cassette series, includes album cover      | $50.14  | $46.75 | $60.31 | $57.29  |
| LAF     | 1–7  | Individual cassettes, includes messages A and B | 6.44    | 6.00   | 7.61   | 7.23    |
| LAF     | SG   | Study guide                                | 5.31    | 4.95   | 6.37   | 6.37    |

*These prices already include the following charges: for delivery in **California,** applicable sales tax; **Canada,** 7% GST and 7% postage and handling (on tapes only); **British Columbia,** 7% GST, 6% British Columbia sales tax (on tapes only), and 7% postage and handling (on tapes only). **The prices are subject to change without notice.**

LAF 1-A: *Your Smile Increases Your Face Value*—A Survey of
Philippians
B: *Set Your Sails for Joy*—Philippians 1:1–11
LAF 2-A: *What a Way to Live!*—Philippians 1:12–21
B: *Laughing through Life's Dilemmas*—Philippians 1:21–30
LAF 3-A: *The Hidden Secret of a Happy Life*—Philippians 2:1–11
B: *While Laughing, Keep Your Balance!*—
Philippians 2:12–18
LAF 4-A: *Friends Make Life More Fun*—Philippians 2:19–30
B: *Happy Hopes for High Achievers*—Philippians 3:1–11
LAF 5-A: *Hanging Tough Together . . . and Loving It*—
Philippians 3:12–16
B: *It's a Mad, Bad, Sad World, But . . .*—
Philippians 3:17–4:1
LAF 6-A: *Defusing Disharmony*—Philippians 4:1–3
B: *Freeing Yourself Up to Laugh Again*—Philippians 4:4–9
LAF 7-A: *Don't Forget to Have Fun as You Grow Up*—
Philippians 4:10–19
B: *A Joyful, Grace-Filled Good-Bye*—Philippians 4:19–23

## How to Order by Mail

Simply mark on the order form whether you want the series or individual tapes. Mail the form with your payment to the appropriate address listed below. We will process your order as promptly as we can.

**United States:** Mail your order to the Listener Services Department at Insight for Living, Post Office Box 69000, Anaheim, California 92817-0900. If you wish your order to be shipped first-class for faster delivery, add 10 percent of the total order amount. Otherwise, please allow four to six weeks for delivery by fourth-class mail. We accept personal checks, money orders, Visa, or MasterCard in payment for materials. Unfortunately, we are unable to offer invoicing or COD orders.

**Canada:** Mail your order to Insight for Living Ministries, Post Office Box 2510, Vancouver, British Columbia V6B 3W7. Allow approximately four weeks for delivery. We accept personal checks, money orders, Visa, or MasterCard in payment for materials. Unfortunately, we are unable to offer invoicing or COD orders.

**Australia, New Zealand, or Papua New Guinea:** Mail your order to Insight for Living, Inc., GPO Box 2823 EE, Melbourne, Victoria 3001, Australia. Please allow six to ten weeks for delivery by surface mail. If you would like your order sent airmail, the delivery time may be reduced. Using the United States price as a base, add postage costs—surface or airmail—to the amount of your order. Please use the chart that follows to determine correct postage. Due to fluctuating currency rates, we can accept only personal checks made payable in U.S. funds, international money orders, Visa, or MasterCard in payment for materials.

**Overseas:** Other overseas residents should mail their orders to our United States office. Please allow six to ten weeks for delivery by surface mail. If you would like your order sent airmail, the delivery time may be reduced. Using the United States price as a base, add postage costs— surface or airmail—to the amount of your order. Please use the chart that follows to determine correct postage. Due to fluctuating currency rates, we can accept only personal checks made payable in U.S. funds, international money orders, Visa, or MasterCard in payment for materials.

| Type of Postage | Postage Cost |
|-----------------|--------------|
| Surface | 10% of total order |
| Airmail | 25% of total order |

## For Faster Service, Order by Telephone or FAX

For Visa or MasterCard orders, you are welcome to use one of our toll-free numbers between the hours of 7:00 A.M. and 4:30 P.M., Pacific time, Monday through Friday, or our FAX numbers. The numbers to use from anywhere in the United States are **1-800-772-8888** or FAX (714) 575-5049. To order from Canada, call our Vancouver office using **1-800-663-7639** or FAX (604) 596-2975. Vancouver residents, call (604) 596-2910. Australian residents should phone (03) 872-4606. From other international locations, call our Listener Services Department at (714) 575-5000 in the United States.

## Our Guarantee

Our cassettes are guaranteed for ninety days against faulty performance or breakage due to a defect in the tape. For best results, please be sure your tape recorder is in good operating condition and is cleaned regularly.

**Note:** To cover processing and handling, there is a $10 fee for *any* returned check.

## Insight for Living Catalog

Request a free copy of the Insight for Living catalog of books, tapes, and study guides by calling **1-800-772-8888** in the United States or **1-800-663-7639** in Canada.

# Order Form

LAF CS represents the entire *Laugh Again* series in a special album cover, while LAF 1–7 are the individual tapes included in the series. LAF SG represents this study guide, should you desire to order additional copies.

| Item | Calif.* | Unit Price U.S. | B.C.* | Canada* | Quantity | Amount |
|------|---------|------|-------|---------|----------|--------|
| LAF CS | $50.14 | $46.75 | $60.31 | $57.29 | | $ |
| LAF 1 | 6.44 | 6.00 | 7.61 | 7.23 | | |
| LAF 2 | 6.44 | 6.00 | 7.61 | 7.23 | | |
| LAF 3 | 6.44 | 6.00 | 7.61 | 7.23 | | |
| LAF 4 | 6.44 | 6.00 | 7.61 | 7.23 | | |
| LAF 5 | 6.44 | 6.00 | 7.61 | 7.23 | | |
| LAF 6 | 6.44 | 6.00 | 7.61 | 7.23 | | |
| LAF 7 | 6.44 | 6.00 | 7.61 | 7.23 | | |
| LAF SG | 5.31 | 4.95 | 6.37 | 6.37 | | |
| | | | | | **Subtotal** | |
| | | **Overseas Residents** *Pay U.S. price plus 10% surface postage or 25% airmail. Also, see "How to Order by Mail."* | | | | |
| | | **U.S. First-Class Shipping** *For faster delivery, add 10% for postage and handling.* | | | | |
| | | **Gift to Insight for Living** *Tax-deductible in the United States and Canada.* | | | | |
| | | **Total Amount Due** *Please do not send cash.* | | | | $ |

If there is a balance: ☐ Apply it as a donation ☐ Please refund
*These prices already include applicable taxes and shipping costs.

**Payment by:** ☐ Check or money order made payable to Insight for Living or

☐ Credit card (circle one): Visa  MasterCard   Number _____

Expiration Date _____ Signature _____
We cannot process your credit card purchase without your signature.

Name _____

Address _____

City _____ State/Province _____

Zip/Postal Code _____ Country _____

Telephone ( ) _____ Radio Station ____ ____ ____ ____
If questions arise concerning your order, we may need to contact you.

**Mail this order form to the Listener Services Department at one of these addresses:**

Insight for Living, Post Office Box 69000, Anaheim, CA 92817-0900
Insight for Living Ministries, Post Office Box 2510, Vancouver, BC, Canada V6B 3W7
Insight for Living, Inc., GPO Box 2823 EE, Melbourne, VIC 3001, Australia

# Order Form

LAF CS represents the entire *Laugh Again* series in a special album cover, while LAF 1–7 are the individual tapes included in the series. LAF SG represents this study guide, should you desire to order additional copies.

| Item | Calif.* | Unit Price U.S. | B.C.* | Canada* | Quantity | Amount |
|------|---------|------|-------|---------|----------|--------|
| LAF CS | $50.14 | $46.75 | $60.31 | $57.29 | | $ |
| LAF 1 | 6.44 | 6.00 | 7.61 | 7.23 | | |
| LAF 2 | 6.44 | 6.00 | 7.61 | 7.23 | | |
| LAF 3 | 6.44 | 6.00 | 7.61 | 7.23 | | |
| LAF 4 | 6.44 | 6.00 | 7.61 | 7.23 | | |
| LAF 5 | 6.44 | 6.00 | 7.61 | 7.23 | | |
| LAF 6 | 6.44 | 6.00 | 7.61 | 7.23 | | |
| LAF 7 | 6.44 | 6.00 | 7.61 | 7.23 | | |
| LAF SG | 5.31 | 4.95 | 6.37 | 6.37 | | |
| | | | | | **Subtotal** | |
| | | | **Overseas Residents** *Pay U.S. price plus 10% surface postage or 25% airmail. Also, see "How to Order by Mail."* | | | |
| | | | **U.S. First-Class Shipping** *For faster delivery, add 10% for postage and handling.* | | | |
| | | | **Gift to Insight for Living** *Tax-deductible in the United States and Canada.* | | | |
| | | | **Total Amount Due** *Please do not send cash.* | | | $ |

If there is a balance: ☐ Apply it as a donation ☐ Please refund
*These prices already include applicable taxes and shipping costs.

**Payment by:** ☐ Check or money order made payable to Insight for Living or

☐ Credit card (circle one): Visa MasterCard Number _____

Expiration Date _____ Signature _____
We cannot process your credit card purchase without your signature.

Name _____

Address _____

City _____ State/Province _____

Zip/Postal Code _____ Country _____

Telephone ( ) _____ Radio Station ___ ___ ___ ___
If questions arise concerning your order, we may need to contact you.

**Mail this order form to the Listener Services Department at one of these addresses:**

Insight for Living, Post Office Box 69000, Anaheim, CA 92817-0900
Insight for Living Ministries, Post Office Box 2510, Vancouver, BC, Canada V6B 3W7
Insight for Living, Inc., GPO Box 2823 EE, Melbourne, VIC 3001, Australia